BLOODY YORKSHIRE

Volume 1

W M RHODES

Also by W M Rhodes

Filey a History of the Town and its People
ISBN: 978-0-9957752-06

Scarborough a History of the Town and its People
978-0-9957752-7-5

Dr Pritchard the Poisoning Adulterer.
978-0-9957752-6-8

ISBN:978-0-9957752-2-0
A copy of this book has been lodged with The British Library.
Edited by Maureen Vincent-Northam
Cover Photograph 'Bolton Abbey' reproduced with the kind
permission of Bob Robertson.
Cover Design - Rhys Vincent-Northam
Book Design -Beenish Qureshi.
Published in the United Kingdom – La-di Dah Publishing.

Table of Contents

Acknowledgements

Thank you to my Grandmother Mary Theresa Leclerc whose passion for murder stories inspired me to write this book.
R.I.P

The stories reconstructed in this book are from actual events.
The information given, and the crimes depicted, are based on legal evidence, statements, eyewitness accounts, court transcripts, newspapers and testimony given by those involved, personal interviews, individual research, and media resources.

INTRODUCTION

Yorkshire is the largest county in the country. Steeped in history this normally peaceful area has occasionally been gripped by some of the most horrifying crimes of the nineteenth century.

'Bloody Yorkshire' chronicles thirteen of the vilest murderous acts, which frame Yorkshire's sinister past.

This carefully researched illustrated book will appeal to historians, and those interested in true crime.

The Police Force

Sir Robert Peel founded the first modern police force in London in 1829, which replaced the disorganised systems of parish councils and wardens. In 1835 all boroughs in England were compelled to form their own force. However, until 1856 it was not compulsory to have a police presence in rural areas, which before then relied on an unpaid parish constable to keep law and order.

The first force of detectives was founded in London in 1842. In 1878 the detective force was reorganised and renamed the Criminal Investigation Department.

Quarter Sessions

In the nineteenth century, there were three types of courts for criminals to be brought to justice. Quarter sessions, Petty Sessions, and Assizes.

The history of quarter sessions can be traced back to 1327 when Edward III appointed men in every county to keep the peace. By 1368 these officers were empowered to hear and determine cases brought to them on criminal matters, and in 1388 they were commanded to sit four times a year in their counties.

Quarter sessions took place on, Epiphany-Winter, Lent-Spring, Summer and Michaelmas-Winter. They were held before a 'bench' which consisted of two or more Justices of the Peace together with a jury (usually local businessmen from the local vicinity). More serious 'capital' cases could be transferred to the Assizes. Often these sessions took place in the local public house or in a schoolroom, as they tended to have a room big enough for these hearings to take place.

Petty Sessions

These sessions tended to hear the less serious cases, such as drunkenness, poaching, vagrancy.

Assizes

Capital offences were heard at the Assizes. These crimes included murder, manslaughter, rape, treason, fraud and theft. The Assizes were radically reformed in 1971 by The Court Acts 1971 and replaced by the Crown Court, and Magistrates Courts.

Punishment for Murder

Death by hanging could be ordered by the Assizes judge, where more serious offences were tried. At the beginning of the Victorian period, executions were carried out in public, and people would travel far and wide to witness the death of a convicted criminal. The Prison Act 1868 made it mandatory that all future prosecutions were to take place privately within the prison walls.

Once a prisoner was convicted of murder the judge would put the black cap on his head, a clear indication that the prisoner was to be hanged. He/she would then be taken to the prison nearest the court to which the hearing was heard and placed in the condemned cell until it was time for him or her to meet their fate.

The alternative to hanging was transportation and penal servitude which meant prisoners were sent to the colonies to serve out their sentence. Anyone with a sentence of seven years and over could be transported. This method of punishment was abolished in 1857.

Prisons in Yorkshire (19th century)

York Castle

Armey Gaol

Wakefield Gaol

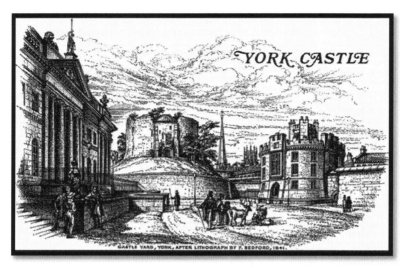

York prison has been a site of justice and incarceration for over one thousand years. William the Conqueror built the first castle in 1068 as a base to control the north of England, it was also used as a gaol.

Clifford's Tower, once the centre of government for the north of England, was built at the same time as the castle. The Assizes court was held here spring/summer. Prisoners awaiting trial were held in the dungeon.

In 1700 the main buildings were knocked down to make way for a county prison for Yorkshire. It opened in 1705 and still stands today. It was known as the debtor's prison and now forms a part of the museum.

A female prison was added in 1780, and in 1835 a third large prison was added next to Clifford's Tower, but it has not survived. It closed in 1929 when it was bought by York council, and demolished.

Armley Gaol

Creative Commons Licence

Leeds Gaol or Armley Jail as it is known locally was built in 1847. The architects were Messrs Perkin & Backhouse and the building was constructed in a Norman style and adapted to reflect strength. Upon each side of the entrance are 'porters lodges,' and over these are the borough arms which are placed in a machicolated parapet.

Initially, the gaol had 480 cells, but a further thirty were added in 1857. It was again extended in 1907.

The prison's first governor was Mr James Paige, who had been deputy governor of Wakefield prison. His appointment attracted a salary of two hundred and fifty pounds a year, together with a free house, coal and gas.

The first prisoners arrived in 1847; there were no beds in the cells, instead, just a thick hammock suspended across the room. There was a small hole in the door to allow food to be passed through. A pull bell was installed in each cell in case of sickness, which if pulled caused a gong to be struck in the main corridor, this flashed up an index plate indicating the number of the cell that required assistance.

Armley started hanging prisoners in 1864 when it took over the execution duties from York Castle. A total of ninety-four criminals were hanged at the prison including one female, Emily Swann, in 1903.

Wakefield Gaol

Wakefield Gaol 1915 Authors own collection

Wakefield Gaol has been a house of correction since 1594. Extended considerably during the Victorian period. It is now the largest high-security prison in the United Kingdom. Nicknamed 'Monster Mansion' due to the detention of some of the country's most depraved and dangerous criminals, such as Ian Huntley, Dr Harold Shipman, Charles Bronson and in the 50's the prison was home to several IRA prisoners.

The nursery rhyme, 'here we go around the mulberry bush' originated in Wakefield Prison in the 1700s. Female prisoners used to exercise around a bush in the exercise yard with their children where they made up the chant as they danced. The tree survives to this day and was shortlisted for the tree of the year in 2016.

In 2001 it was announced that a new Supermax security unit was to be built at Wakefield Prison. The unit was to house the most dangerous inmates within the British prisons system and was the first such unit of its kind to be built in the United Kingdom.

*

1

THE MURDER OF JANE ROBINSON — ESKDALESIDE CUM UGGLEBARNBY — 1841

At a little after 8 o'clock on the morning of the 8th September 1841, farmer John Robinson left his farm in the quiet, peaceful village of Eskdaleside to go to Egton Fair. His servants were busy working in the field on the harvest, and his wife Jane was alone in the house tending to her domestic duties.

The servants returned to the house at noon expecting their lunch, what they found was a horrifying scene – their mistress lying lifeless on the kitchen floor, on her side, with her face towards the ground surrounded by a pool of blood. One brave servant regained his composure and turned the body over to find that his mistress' head was almost severed from her body, which was stiff and rigid.

Drawers and cupboards in the kitchen were broken into and the house ransacked, with bloody fingerprints of the perpetrator's guilt found on various pieces of furniture which had been touched during the pilfering. It was discovered that 32 gold sovereigns were missing together with a box belonging to one of the servants including a pocketbook and silver.

Meanwhile, Mr Robinson finished his business in Egton and was about to saddle his horse to return home, when he was met by one of his servants who had the distressing job of delivering the devastating news of the murders. Horrified, Mr Robinson and the servant went directly to Whitby and informed the police.

Superintendent Mr Wilkinson, the head of Whitby Police together with two police officers hastily attended the dreadful scene.

Mr Wilkinson and his vigilant officers soon carried out their initial inquiries and discovered that two suspicious characters of Irish descent were seen hovering around the house earlier the same morning that the foul murder was committed.

The missing servant's pocketbook and the box it was locked in was found tossed in a field on the road to Lythe. The investigating officers wasted no time in pursuing and apprehending these two men, who in their defence stated that they were Irish reapers seeking employment in the town of Mickleby as they had worked there the previous autumn. Mr Wilkinson was not happy with their explanations and felt justified in transferring the pair to Whitby for further enquiries.

Several farmers came forward to confirm the Irishmen's stories. Both these men were found to be quiet and inoffensive and were exonerated from police inquiries.

In such a quiet place as Eskerdale, it was unthinkable to believe that a stranger could be responsible for such a horrendous slaying. Mr Robinson, the deceased's husband was a 61year-old farmer and well-respected within the community. Fortunately, for him, he had a motive and several people vouched to have seen him at Egton. He was not under any suspicion.

The police were baffled and were under the impression that whoever had committed this ghastly murder was conversant not only with the area but with the house and the Robinsons themselves. An inquest into the murder was held at the Tunnel Inn before John Buchannan Esq Coroner, assisted by magistrates John Chapman and Mr Richardson.

At the inquest, police revealed that the night before the murder the perpetrator slept in an outhouse adjoining Robinson's house, as they had uncovered newly cut ash-stick there. Furthermore, a tile outside the kitchen door had been moved to allow the murderer to have a clearer view of the kitchen. The murderer must have cut their hand carrying out this foul deed, as prints were found on a discarded silver plate that had been dropped nearby. A reward of two hundred pounds was offered to apprehend the offender.

Initially, a man named George Ward was a suspect and his description was issued in the Police Gazette. Ward surrendered to the police, but he had a perfect alibi and was released without charge. He also denied all previous charges against him for other crimes, based on information received from a man named Swales who, for some reason, had a grudge against Ward, and who, by putting Ward's name forward for this murder, was hoping to claim the reward money.

Another man named Tewart of Kirkbymoorside was brought in for questioning, he too was discharged. Tewart had been seen walking near the lane on the morning of the murder and was acquainted with the Robinson family, having been in the habit of calling at the farm for butter and eggs when he was working on the nearby Ironstone quarry. Tewart had called at the Robinson's recently to inquire about a man named Swales. Tewart had left the area shortly afterwards raising police suspicions.

Following their instincts, the police travelled to Kirkbymoorside to speak to Tewart. They first spoke to his father-in-law who showed them where the suspect lived. They knocked on the door, but the father-in-law said, 'they must all be in bed!' The door was then opened rather aggressively be the man's wife who coarsely asked the police what they wanted. The father-in-law panicked and shouted to his daughter 'don't let them in they are after your husband!'

The wife then replied, 'you have had a wasted journey, he's not here, he's gone to live in County Durham!'

The conduct of the father-in-law perplexed the police and fuelled their suspicions, they were convinced that something was amiss. So, they arrested him and travelled to County Durham to detain their original suspect, Mr Tewart.

The people of the small quiet area of Eskdaleside were in an uproar, how could such a brutal crime have been committed without anybody seeing anything? Rumours were rife, and anonymous letters pointing fingers of suspicion poured in daily to the police station. Malicious and false statements were fabricated, some purely in the hope of gaining the reward money, all of which did no more than to divert suspicion away from whomever the real murderer was.

The public demanded an arrest, but nothing was happening. When the police returned from Durham a large crowd gathered outside the train station expecting the murderer to be brought by rail. They were disappointed.

The last person to see Mrs Robinson alive was Mr William Hill, a miller from Thurndale who had for many years supplied the Robinsons with meal. He had called on Mrs Robinson on the day of her murder, but he said that he had left her in good spirits at ten o'clock in the morning.

The surgeon who examined the body gave his opinion that Mrs Robinson met her tragic death before this time. At the time no one had suspected Mr Hill, he was trusted and popular within the community. On that fateful morning, Mr Hill for some reason had taken a different path home to his usual route, which raised suspicion. Mr Hill was apprehended. Under questioning at the police station, Mr Hill became agitated and made incomplete and unsatisfactory statements. According to his statement, Mr Hill had told the Robinsons that he was unable to grind the oats for the pig as he normally did, on that day he was in a rush to get home, but that he would call and do them on Friday. So, why did Mr Hill take the long walk home as opposed to his usual route? Could it be because he needed to gain his composure and remove traces of guilt following the terrible act he had committed on Mrs Robinson?

Under questioning, Hill was asked, 'why did you take a long way home and not the path you usually took? We do know that you left Iburnside at eight in the morning, you made two calls and returned home at eleven-thirty so what did you do in this time? You were seen proceeding at a rapid pace up Fair Head Lane by some of Mr Robinson's servants, and again by servants of Mr Buttery working in the field opposite, who all confirm the time they saw you come in contact with Mr Wilson and ask him if there was any firewood worth taking. You go off for your cart but are not seen with any firewood.'

Hill could not offer any answers that would satisfy the enquiries.

Dr Merryweather was adamant that Mrs Robinson met her death before ten in the morning, so Hill must have been present at that time. Moreover, a sack of oats was found at the scene tied with the deceased's garter and this sack was stained with blood. Again, this raised suspicions, especially as Hill, was in such a hurry to rush off home.

On the 27th November 1841, Mr Hill was committed to York Castle to stand trial for the murder of Jane Robinson. At his trial, the magistrates and members of the jury were not satisfied that the evidence against Hill was strong enough to imply his involvement in the murder. He was subsequently released from custody with no further charge.

Mr Hill returned home, but suspicion surrounding him did not go away, many people still believe that he was guilty. Consequently, he was hounded both mentally and physically by the local community.

FINAL EXAMINATION AND COMMITTAL OF THE SUSPECTED MURDERER.

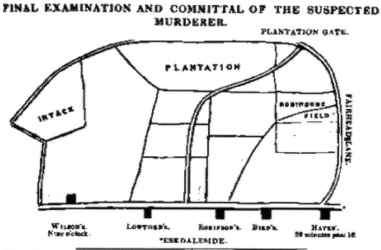

Plan of the relative position of the Premises mentioned in the following Account, and of the Route taken by HILL, the Accused.

The Marquis of Normandy was staying at Mulgrave Castle which is only ten miles from where this barbaric murder occurred. He was desperate to allay the bad feeling that existed in the town, so much so that he intervened, and demanded an interview with the Chief Commissioner of Police in London. On the instructions of the Commissioner, Inspector Nicholas Pearce was appointed to lead the investigation, which was to become the first case in which an officer from Scotland Yard was sent to investigate serious crime in the provinces.

Pearce had recently been involved in bringing the murderer Courvoisier to justice and had a great deal of experience in the police force.

Pearce first went to Whitby in plain clothes and mingled amongst the locals hoping to hear some loose tongues uttering secrets. He worked alone and took a systematic, objective approach and he quickly familiarised himself with all aspects of the murder including visiting the crime scene and studying all the evidence. Pearce was soon of the opinion that Hill was indeed innocent and looked elsewhere for clues to find the real culprit.

Pearce was convinced that the man responsible had hidden in the outhouse twenty yards from the house carefully watching the Robinson's family's movements. Pearce also discovered that on the day of the murder a man dressed in a blue cloth cap, white shooting jacket, and dark trousers had been seen passing the wood where the servant's notebook had been found, together with a piece of bread which was made from a certain recipe only found in that area. The police were convinced that the murderer had thrown these items there.

Inspector Pearce questioned Mary Frankish, one of Robinson's servant girls, who confirmed that on the Sunday prior to the murder, she had seen a man laying down on the grass by the side of the railroad close to Robinson's farm. Mary recognised him as Thomas Redhead who had worked for the Robinsons at one time. Redhead told her that the reason for his visit was that he was on his way to see a Mr John Hodgson of Goathland who he had previously lived with.

However, instead of doing this Redhead accompanied the girl to her uncle's house in Goathland. Frankish agreed to lend him some money, despite him already owing her 40 shillings from the last time they worked together. Redhead convinced her that he had been left some money by his brother and he would return the loan as soon as he went to the bank in Whitby. She never saw him again.

After enquiries, Inspector Pearce discovered that Redhead had arrived in the area via the Stockton coach. Pearce went to the poor rates office in Stockton and found that Redhead had died of Smallpox in 1842. Pearce then travelled to Sheldon and found a pitman named Bland who Redhead had lived with prior to his death. Bland confirmed that Redhead had visited Whitby to withdraw money left to him from his brother and that he did not return to work until all his money was spent.

After this time, he went to work as an excavator on the Shildon Tunnel. Bland said when he returned from Whitby Redhead had repaid several old debts, he also bought many things and even put a 20% deposit down on a grocer's shop in Shildon, going into partnership with a man named Tomlinson. Bland confirmed that when Redhead left for Whitby, he was wearing a blue cloth cap, white jacket, dark trousers and he returned in the same attire.

It seems that Redhead's choice of a business partner was misguided as Tomlinson was also a dubious character; as soon as the partners took possession of the shop Tomlinson turfed Redhead out without a penny. Redhead commenced legal proceedings but was not fit enough to see the proceedings through. The case was abandoned. From then on Redhead, it was said, would walk around the town with his head down never looking anyone in the eye, and although he did return to work, he refused to speak to any of his work colleagues.

Pearce became convinced that Redhead's partner Tomlinson must have known about the murder and was an accomplice to it. Pearce arrested him, but Tomlinson swore that he knew nothing about it. Without any evidence, Pearce released him without charge.

Prior to his death Redhead went back to live at Bland's house after first living briefly with a Mrs Brown. Mrs Brown informed the police that she had visited Redhead at Mr Bland's house at the beginning of January, where she found him ill in bed with smallpox. Redhead was very ill, distressed, and constantly crying. Mrs Brown said he grabbed hold of her hand and tried to tell her something muttering to her 'I must tell you – I must', but he couldn't say what he wanted to say, the words seemed to choke him. He died soon after without confessing to Mrs Brown. Mrs Brown told the inspector that she thought Redhead had died of a broken heart.

Inspector Pearce found Redhead's pocketbook and, on the date the murder took place, the diary had a few drops of blood on it. These facts left no doubt in the inspector's mind that Redhead was indeed the murderer of Mrs Jane Robinson. Whitby magistrates agreed, and Pearce was highly complimented for the skills he had portrayed.

2

THE MURDER HOUSE — THE TRIPLE MURDERS AT WATER ROYD HOUSE MIRFIELD — 1847

The Murder House' Water Royd House. Picture credit Gary Peacock.

One of the country's vilest and inexplicable murders happened in the picturesque town of Mirfield on 12th May 1847, where three people – an elderly couple and their servant girl – were brutally butchered to death without provocation. The crime happened around lunchtime at Water Royd House, the residence of the victims Mr and Mrs Wraith and their servant girl twenty-year-old Caroline Ellis. James Wraith was seventy-seven and his wife Ann sixty-five.

A retired, well-respected gentleman Mr Wraith had worked as a steward for many years to Samuel Brook Esq and Joseph Ingham of

Blake Hall. He was not a rich man, but he was shrewd with his money and a good businessman. Water Royd House was a smallholding with seven acres of land; Wraith also owned several smaller cottages in Outwood, Wakefield, which he rented out. A few weeks before his murder Mr Wraith had sold some properties, it was unclear if the money from the sales of these houses was in the house, and that robbery was the intended motive for this atrocity.

Water Royd House sat in a secluded position, standing back from the road behind the Zion Baptist Church (now demolished) and surrounded by fields and footpaths. The only way to the house was via a private lane to the back of the property. The house was built of substantial stone with two parlours and a kitchen on the ground floor and three bedrooms on the first floor.

Mr Wraith had been married twice; his first wife Mary had died some years before. James had no children, but he did have nephews and relatives in the neighbourhood; one of them, the Green family, lived just across the lane at Cripplegate. His second wife Ann had two sons from her previous marriage and owned property in her own right that she rented out. One of her sons lived in Leeds the other, a schoolmaster, lived not far from his mother at Mirfield. This son for one reason or another found it difficult to make ends meet, so his mother supplied him with a weekly subsidy of one pound, a transaction that her husband found difficult to accept.

The servant girl Caroline Ellis, the daughter of James and Jemima Ellis, was a young local girl who had worked for the Wraiths for a year and was due to get married on Sunday 16th May (the day after she was laid to rest). The custom in those days was that women would not work outside the home when they married so it was most likely that Caroline was working out her notice when she was brutally murdered.

On the day of the murder, James Wraith was last seen around midday going across the road at Cripplegate to ask for help from his great-nephew Joshua Green to move some stone on his land that afternoon. Just over an hour later thirteen-year-old Joshua went to Water Royd House to start the work. On his arrival, he found the doors locked and the blinds of the windows down. More alarmingly Joshua was shocked to see blood oozing from under the front door. Terrified, he quickly retreated to tell his mother what he had seen.

In Joshua's own words 'I went to the front door, and saw blood running out, bubbling up – lumps like.'

Joshua running out of the house after the gruesome discovery. Credit Gary Peacock.

Joshua's mother sent his older brother Thomas back to the house and dashed across the road to fetch John McKinnell who kept The King's Head pub at the end of the lane. John McKinnell accompanied Thomas to the house. The door was locked and, unusually, there was no key to the other side of the door.

McKinnell managed to open the kitchen window, then the shutters, and climbed in, followed by young Thomas Green. They were shocked at what greeted them; it was a terrifying, gruesome sight. They found Caroline Ellis lying on the floor of the kitchen on her back with her head towards the door, her teeth and bits of her brain lay on the floor and her feet spread towards the fire fender. She was dead but still warm. Her throat had been cut and her skull broken, a pool of blood pooled around her head.

From the kitchen, McKinnell went into the passage, which ran between the two front rooms. In the passage, he found Ann Wraith, her head laid against the front door, a pool of blood about her head, her right eye was smashed from its socket, and she also had her throat cut and her skull broken.

James Wraith was found in the interior of the dining room lying on the floor, his throat had also been slashed and he had a razor at his breast.

Drawers and cabinets were ransacked, and a silver tankard smeared in blood was on the table, there was beer at the bottom of this cup which was tainted with blood. Mr Wraith must have been interrupted during his lunch as a plate containing a partly eaten meat pie was on the table, together with two knives and forks and two German silver spoons. Under the table was another plate which Mrs Wraith was in the habit of leaving out with dinner-scraps for her beloved cats.

A poker, which must have been used in the slaying, was found in the dining room. The weapon was bent and slung on the floor. It seems that this murdering fiend was not content with fiercely slashing the throats of these poor innocent victims, as after they were dead, he thrust the point of the poker repeatedly into their flesh and kicked them in the most sensitive parts of their bodies.

John McKinnell immediately sent word to fetch the local constable and the surgeon from Mirfield, no one else could enter the house until they arrived.

Superintendent Green and the investigators initially thought that it was James Wraith who did the terrible deed then killed himself, but on closer examination, it was found that he had been knocked down by a blow to the head breaking his jawbone. It was also found that Miss Ellis, a strong, active young woman had been felled to the ground and suffered numerous wounds to her head.

The late Mr and Mrs Wraith were cat lovers and the couple had three cats who, since the murders, had seemingly disappeared. Traumatised by fear they were found some days later huddled together under one of the beds; when found they were petrified and hurriedly made their escape; they were never seen again.

In the mid-nineteenth century prejudice in England was rife and Irish immigrants were treated as 'the criminal class' thus when a crime was committed, they were most likely the first ones to be questioned. In this case, two Irish hawkers were seen in the vicinity of the Wraiths' house around the time of the murders. They were not seen together but were spotted separately a short distance from each other. A man's shirt which was covered in blood was also discovered at Ravensworth about two miles from the scene.

McCabe and Reid were strong, active men, both were married with connections to Water Royd House. Michael McCabe lived at Hightown, Liversedge with his wife Mary and two infant sons – James who was a cripple, and John. McCabe had been near Water Royd House hawking pots and pans; suspicions were raised so the police took him into custody for further questioning. A woman came forward saying that McCabe had been to her house around 1 o'clock on the day of the murder.

McCabe confirmed that he had called on the Wraiths and the door was opened by a young man of about twenty-years-old. The young man said that they didn't need any pots and pans just now. The police were unsure of McCabe and doubted his explanation of the events, especially as the police had found specks of blood on McCabe's boots.

No money was found in the house. In addition, Caroline Ellis's earrings had been torn from her ears, a watch belonging to Mr Wraith was missing as was his wife's ring which had been removed from her finger. The police suspected that robbery was the real motive for the murders.

Superintendent Green apprehended Patrick Reid at his father's home – a lodging house at Daw-Green. Reid, a recently married man with a young child, was a knife and razor grinder by trade and a hawker of pots and pans. When apprehended the police noticed spots of blood on his clothes. It transpired that Reid had previously been banned from the Wraiths' house after an earlier altercation involving Caroline Ellis whereby Reid had accused her of stealing a teapot from him. Mr Wraith told him in no uncertain terms never to come near the house again. So why he was near the house at all was questionable. Reid was taken to a lockup at Dewsbury and charged with the murders of Mr and Mrs Wraith and Caroline Ellis.

Following the murders, Mrs Wraith's son Mr Parker occupied the house. There was no such thing as a protected crime scene in 1847. The floors of the house had been thoroughly scrubbed to remove traces of blood, but there remained spots of blood splatter on the walls and the ceiling which bore testimony to the violence of the blows inflicted by the assassin.

Mr Parker had for a short time opened the house to the macabre and morbidly curious members of the public, who traipsed through the house with weird, morose fascination. In one day, a total of one thousand people walked around. The garden itself had been trampled on so much it resembled a turnpike road. Shrubs, evergreens and even single leaves had been removed from the gardens as ghoulish souvenirs of the terrible atrocity.

McCabe continued to protest his innocence. He gave the statement that he had gone to the Wraiths' back door and had heard footsteps on the stairs. He knocked but no one answered, he knocked again, and he thought he heard a dreadful groaning sound, then the sound of someone coming down the stairs and walking towards the fireplace in the kitchen before walking slowly towards the back door. The back door opened, and McCabe rattled his pots and asked the man if he wanted anything. The man replied, 'No Sir.' McCabe described the man as good looking and around twenty to twenty-five years old. He had seen him around hawking his goods, but he didn't know him to talk to. The man was wearing a jacket with festoon sleeves.

McCabe then went to a friend's house, where strangely enough he didn't mention what he had seen at the Wraiths to his friends or to anyone else. He later declared that he thought Mrs Wraith must have been killing fowls for the Mirfield feast; this he assumed was the reason for the bloody floors or perhaps the noise he heard was Mr and Mrs Wraith were quarrelling. He didn't want them to think he gossiped or they may not order anything from him again, but at no time did he consider murder. He then went to the Shoulder of Mutton pub when he heard talk about the Wraiths – someone had looked through the window and found Mrs Wraith lying dead on the floor. Disturbingly, McCabe kept quiet.

Both prisoners, Reid and McCabe, were remanded in custody pending further investigations.

The Kings Head, Mirfield

On Thursday 13th May 1847, Mr GD Baker deputy-coroner of Wakefield opened the inquest, which was held at The Kings Head, Mirfield in front of a large crowd anxious to see the murderers brought to justice. Michael McCabe was brought before the Coroner and informed of the charges against him. He appeared perfectly calm and listened attentively to the evidence. On this occasion, the inquest was adjourned to 27th May to allow time for the city chemist to analyses the shoes and clothing of the prisoner.

In the meantime, a key was discovered which opened the back door to the Wraiths' house. Witness Jonathan Ashton from Mirfield, said he was asked to climb down the well where he found a soldering iron and a key. The iron had a broken handle. After investigation traces of flesh and muscle were found on the iron.

EAST OR BACK VIEW OF THE RESIDENCE OF THE LATE MR. JAMES WRAITH FINDING OF THE SOLDERING IRON AND KEY IN THE WELL.

In the house, there was blood splattered on the walls and on the ceiling. It seems that Caroline Ellis was cleaning the fireplace and must have been attacked by surprise and struck viciously on the back of her head. She put up a fight as she had bruises on her hands and fingers.

It seems that Reid did not get on with Caroline Ellis, in fact, he hated her. He believed that she had once stolen a tea caddy from his basket and Reid had said to her 'I will revenge of you, at one time or another, you mark my words.' At the time Reid had refused to leave the house. Ellis said if he didn't leave, then she would fetch the police. Hence the reason why Mr Wraith banned Reid from the house.

Caroline Ellis was young and a bit of a gossip and had on occasions told people about Mr Wraith's fortune, which in a cash-strapped small-town where news travelled fast robbery, was probably the motive for the murders.

Another witness gave evidence to say that Reid had asked 'what do you call that servant girl that lives at the Wraiths'?' when asked why he wanted to know Reid said, 'because she's a bitch.'

The adjourned inquest reopened at 11 am on Thursday 27th May 1847, at the Kings Arms. The room soon proved too small and the hearing moved to large premises at the schoolroom belonging to the Wesleyan Chapel.

The first witness called was Martha Ann Lockwood. She said that she lived in Lee Green, Mirfield and that she had been the servant to the Wraiths up to the eighteen months prior to the murder, then a young girl from Thornhill, Hannah Brooks replaced her, followed by one of the Wraiths' relatives called Elizabeth Green. After that, it was Caroline Ellis.

Mrs Lockwood said she knew Patrick Reid; he was a hawker who called at the Wraiths' house once a week. She recalled that there was no quarrel between the parties while she worked there.

Another witness was a neighbour of Reid's father, Mr Thomas Kilty. Kilty testified that he had once borrowed a soldering iron from Reid's father. On the morning of the murder, Patrick Reid had called at the Kilty house asking for it back. Kilty asked if he could borrow it again as there was a rumour flying around that people from Dewsbury were stirring up trouble against the Irish immigrants in Mirfield and that there was going to be a lot of violence in Daw Green after the upcoming Mirfield Feast. Reid told Kilty that his father needed the iron for a job.

Superintendent Green gave evidence on the statement given by Reid when he was apprehended; 'I was at the Wraiths' house with my basket selling my things. I knocked at the door, but no one answered, so I walked away and moved on. The Wraiths is the last house on my round. When there was no answer, I walked down the footpath between the Wraiths' garden and the fields until I came to the town centre. I then crossed over a stile into a field where there is a footpath that leads to Mirfield church where I saw a woman with a basket hawking goods. I waited till she caught me up and we walked together towards the churchyard. We parted when she called in the public house, and I went home past Mr Hague's the magistrate's house, then on to my father's lodging house at Daw Green.'

When asked if he knew who the woman was that he walked with he responded, 'Yes, it was my mother.'

The officer confirmed that when Reid was apprehended, he had taken away items of his clothing for further analysis, namely a dark green coat, and fustian trousers. There were marks on all items that looked like blood. When he asked Reid about the marks he had replied, 'Oh no it will not be blood.' Upstairs in Reid's room, his hawker's basket was recovered, which had a piece of brown paper in it again smeared with blood. There were two baskets in the room, one of which Reid's mother said was hers.

John Leadbeater, a police constable from Mirfield, gave evidence to the enquiry describing how the soldering iron and back door key belonging to Water Royd House was found down the well belonging to the Wraiths' house. 'I pumped the water out of the well. It is a draw well which opened at the top and it is around twelve feet deep. I sent the boy Jonathan Ashton down, then we sent a bucket down and the boy found a key and an iron which he sent back up. The key, by the looks of it, had not been down the well very long, as there was no evidence of rust on either, however, traces of blood were found on the handle of the iron and on the key. We tried the key in the back door, and it worked.'

A variety of witnesses came forward to say they had seen Reid and McCabe in the vicinity of the Wraiths' house around twelve-thirty to one o'clock. However, none of the witnesses said they saw the men together.

Marmaduke Shepley testified: 'I saw Patrick Reid walk down the footpath near the Wraiths' house. I spoke to him saying 'It's a fine day'. Reid replied, 'yes very'. I heard no noise at all from the Wraiths' house.'

Harriet Webster confirmed that she had also seen Reid near the Wraiths' house on the day of the murders. She would recognise him anywhere as in her opinion Reid was the best-looking man she had ever seen.

Hannah Hallas confirmed she had seen and spoken to McCabe. He had a basket of hawker's pots which he carried on his head. He told Mrs Hallas and her mother that he would try a couple of houses, then call on the Wraiths before he went home.

However, there was bad news for McCabe as surgeon Mr Watkinson said that when he examined the body of Caroline Ellis, he noticed that one of her garters was missing. He had seen a garter like the one the dead girl was wearing in the bedroom of McCabe. Miss Esther Lambert, a schoolmistress at the Gray Coat girls' school in York, gave evidence that in her expert opinion the garter found at the McCabe's house matched the knitting on Caroline Ellis' garter and had to have been knitted by the same person and were most likely part of a pair. Furthermore, the bloody shirt found earlier had been destroyed by the woman who found it.

At the fourth and final hearing before deciding if there was enough evidence against the prisoners to send them to trial at the Assizes. No new evidence was brought forward to make the chain of circumstantial evidence stronger than what was already known. After a short recess, Reid was asked if he would like to make a statement. He said that he had nothing further to add except to reaffirm his innocence. Regarding McCabe he was committed to trial on a coroner's warrant, however, his lawyer confirmed that his client now wanted to give evidence on oath against Reid. This hearing was to be heard on July 1847.

At this hearing, McCabe said that he lived in Hightown. He had lived there with his wife and two children for about a month, but he had lived in the area for five years. He knew Mr and Mrs Wraith as he had sold them bit and bats on previous occasions. However, he had not called on them for over a year prior to the date of the murders. He gave the same account as to how he had seen Reid opening the door and then seeing the blood on the floor.

Reid's defence barrister Mr William Digby Seymour argued his client's innocence for almost three hours contending that there was insufficient evidence against Reid. Patrick Reid signed a statement declaring his innocence.

His Lordship went through the evidence and summed up the case in two and a half hours. The jury deliberated and came back after a couple of hours with a question for his Lordship, which they put in writing.

Having read the note, His Lordship asked a jury member to read the note out loud, its content read: The jury would like to know if the prisoner is acquitted of the murder of James Wraith can he afterwards be tried again for the two women, should further evidence be found?

A rather exasperated judge responded in a frustrated tone: 'This is not a question, gentleman, which you can take into consideration, nor any right to entertain. You have only one duty to perform, to consider the case in evidence. You must act upon the evidence before you and reach a conclusion as to the innocence or guilt of the party accused of the murder of James Wraith.'

'Sorry, Judge, but we think there is insufficient evidence for us to reach a conclusion at all.'

'I am sorry to hear that,' said the judge, 'I am afraid I cannot help you.'

The confused juror responded with an extraordinary retort.

'Some of the members of the jury do not know whether we are trying the case on the murder of James Wraith only, or all three people!'

'Then you have greatly misunderstood the case, you are to decide only as to the murder of James Wraith!'

'In that case, we are agreed on a verdict.'

'This is all very well,' the judge directed in a firm voice, 'but bearing in mind what has just happened I ask that you retire to deliberate once more on your findings.'

The jury retired only to return five minutes later; their verdict was 'Not Guilty.'

However, Justice Wightman directed that the two indictments on the murder of Caroline Ellis should stand over to the next hearing, which was held on Monday 20th December 1847 at York Castle. A new jury was sworn in. Counsel for the prosecution Mr Ingham, Mr Overend, Mr Pickering. For McCabe Mr Jackson of York, for Patrick Reid Mr William Digby Seymour. The judge was Mr Justice Patterson.

A large crowd had gathered at the gates all wanting to gain admission to the Castle, as soon as the gates opened a rush ensued and every accessible place in court was immediately filled. After the jury had been sworn in the charges against the prisoners were read out. Patrick Reid was charged with the wilful murder of Caroline Ellis. Michael McCabe for aiding, abetting and assisting Patrick Reid to commit murder. Both prisoners pleaded 'Not Guilty.'

The judge addressed the jury, 'The charges are that the prisoners did, on 12th May 1847, with malice aforethought, murder Caroline Ellis. They have both pleaded not guilty. Your duty is to hear the evidence and to declare whether they are guilty or not.'

Suspicion remained strong against McCabe despite him testifying against Reid at a previous hearing, with the consensus amongst the legal profession that he was at least guilty of *particeps criminis*. Therefore, it was decided that in the hope of gaining further evidence, the indictments for Mrs Wraith and Caroline Ellis should not be disposed of, but postponed. However, at the December Assizes instead of proceeding on those indictments, two fresh bills were presented to the

Grand Jury and Reid was charged on the principal charge (murder) and Michael McCabe, charged with being present at the time of the murders, thus aiding and abetting in the murder of Caroline Ellis and Mrs Ann Wraith. However, both Reid and McCabe were put on trial for the murder of Caroline Ellis.

Two witnesses testified that they had seen both Reid and McCabe going towards the Wraiths' house on the day of the murder. Mary Hallas, a young girl, had come forward with new evidence, confirming that she had seen both men in the oat field near Water Royd House. Mary Hallas had been kept back previously from saying what she had witnessed as her parents did not want her involved.

Benjamin Morton, a hawker from Nab Lane, testified that he knew both Reid and McCabe and that on the day of the murders he had seen both men within sixty yards of each other, he said that they both had baskets with them. Morton had not seen Reid's face, but he knew it was him.

After a long and patient enquiry where the evidence was repeated in a similar fashion to the previous hearings the prosecution, Mr William Digby Seymour, addressed the jury for his client Patrick Reid and contended 'that the evidence did not substantiate the case against his client and that McCabe was the real murderer and that the fresh evidence given by Mary Hallas did not alter the position of Reid from that in which he was acquitted at the last assizes.'

Mr Mathews (McCabe's defence lawyer) then addressed the jury for McCabe contending that although his client was at the house at the time of the murder Michael McCabe did not commit this dreadful atrocity; he was simply unfortunate to be in the wrong place at the wrong time.

On 24th December the learned judge started his summing up, a task that took over three hours. He went through the evidence explaining how it affected each prisoner, more especially with McCabe, detailing that if the timings were correct then the girl Hallas cannot have seen the prisoners together. Also, there was no evidence to suggest that the prisoners knew each other and that it was against all probability that two strangers would commit such a vicious murder.

The jury retired to consider the evidence. They returned some two hours later with a verdict of 'Guilty' against both men. His Lordship then put on the black cap, and after alluding to the cruel and horrid way in which the murders had been perpetrated, urged the despicable men to make the best of the time they had left, and to prepare themselves for the next world. He then pronounced the sentence of death on each prisoner.

Reid continued to retain his calmness throughout the sentence, but it was all too much for McCabe who fainted when hearing the judge's words, and the hearing stopped until he could be revived.

In a most surprising turn of events immediately after the trial, Patrick Reid's lawyer came forward to the judge to say that his client had made a full confession exonerating McCabe completely.

Reid's confession was that; 'on 12th May 1847, I had gone to the Wraiths' house around twenty-five minutes to one. I conversed with the servant girl for a short time, I then took the soldering iron out of my basket and struck Caroline Ellis over the back of her head. She shrieked out and staggered to the back door, I struck her again and she felled to the floor.

'Mr Wraith then came up from the cellar with a tankard of beer in his hand. I struck him a violent blow to his head with the iron, in doing so the handle of the iron flew off with the force of the blow. Mr Wraith staggered to the parlour. I then grabbed the kitchen poker and ran into the passage where I saw Mrs Wraith running towards the front door. I stopped her and struck her two or three blows to the head. She fell to the ground. I then returned to the parlour where Mr Wraith lay bleeding on the floor insensible. I rifled his pockets and took his keys out and I opened the drawers with them. I then heard a knock on the kitchen door, at first, I thought it was Caroline Ellis getting up, but I checked her, and she was perfectly still.

'I opened the door slightly and saw McCabe who asked if I wanted anything in his line. I said, no. I wasn't too concerned about McCabe as I thought that he was a stranger and would not recognise me. I then shut and bolted the door. I then had good luck around the house, and I found a box with razors in it. I took out a razor and slashed the throats of all three people. I then left the house and locked the kitchen door and threw the key and the soldering iron down the well. I then hurried towards my own house.'

Reid's written confession. Credit Gary Peacock

McCabe confronted Reid asking him directly: 'Did I have anything whatsoever to do with these murders?' To which Reid responded: 'No, you didn't, if I thought you had known anything about it, I would have murdered you too, you've brought all this on yourself with all the false statements you made about the whole affair.'

Reid's countenance to his fate evinced great calmness; he immediately appeared to resign himself to his fate, whereas McCabe was greatly affected by the verdict and was unable to bear up.

Despite Reid's counsel William Digby Seymour knowing of his confession prior to the trial in December, there was nothing to be done as to the fate of McCabe, as the judge had already passed the sentence. It was up to the secretary of state Sir George Grey to determine whether the confession of Reid could be relied upon. A statement at the time suggested, that it was not improbable that McCabe's life would be spared and there is the possibility that he would be dealt with as an accessory after the fact.

After his condemnation, Patrick Reid was frequently visited by his friends and family. He left a father, mother, wife and infant child. Reid's mother suffered greatly for her son's crimes, she was in a state of utter destitution, shunned by all and pitied by none. Reid was so concerned about his mother at that time that he wrote to Reverend Edward O'Neil of Dewsbury reaffirming his confession that he alone was responsible for the murders. He said that he was aware that many people were blaming his mother and that she had encouraged him in this foul deed. On the contrary, he said, if his parents – especially his mother – had known of his intentions, then they would have put a stop to it, and he would not be facing the hangman now. He asked if the Reverend could stop the condemnation of his mother, saying that she had to bear the pain of losing her son.

Saturday 8th January 1848, Patrick Reid faced the ultimate penalty of the law for his atrocious crimes. So intense was the interest in this case that many thousands of people came from far and wide to York to witness Reid's public execution, extra train carriages were put on especially for the occasion with every seat taken.

Between eleven and twelve o'clock the operation of the pinioning commenced. Reid was brought forth and the mournful procession started.

Reid walked with utmost calmness and composure to the scaffold. He knelt and engaged in prayer then he arose and crossed his breast. He then turned around and addressed those immediately around him and in a clear voice said; 'Well gentlemen, I wish to say that I alone am the guilty person; that McCabe is entirely innocent, and that no human being in the entire world had anything to do with it but myself.'

The executioner, Nathaniel Howard, tied the noose loosely so instead of breaking his neck Reid was strangled and it took a painful two hours for him to die.

On the 1st February 1848 the secretary of state revealed McCabe's fate in a letter from Whitehall, which read;

> "Whitehall, 1st February, 1848.
>
> "Sir,—I am directed by Secretary Sir George Grey to acknowledge the receipt of your letter of the 27th ult., respecting the case of Michael M'Cabe, who was convicted at the Winter Assizes holden for the county of York in December last of murder, and sentenced to death. And I am to acquaint you that, since the trial, the case of M'Cabe has been frequently under the consideration of the Judge before whom the prisoner was tried, and he is of opinion that M'Cabe was a participator in the crime, to a certain extent, and has recommended that his sentence should be commuted to transportation for life, and that Sir George Grey has thereupon recommended the prisoner to her Majesty for the grant of a pardon upon that condition.
>
> "I am, Sir, your obedient servant,
>
> "S. M. PHILLIPS.

The letter was communicated to Michael McCabe who was extremely disappointed, and much affected by its content. McCabe continued to declare his innocence. His solicitor avowed that further efforts would be made to secure his release. Unfortunately, this did not happen, and despite Reid's dying confession which was considered by all to be an honest and true one, and that Reid alone committed the crimes. It made no difference to McCabe's fate, and he was sent to fulfil his sentence in Australia.

So why was McCabe given such a harsh sentence even though he was innocent of these crimes? Why did he not receive a free pardon?

It can be argued that the case against Michael McCabe is one of the worst cases of miscarriages of justice ever known in the United Kingdom. The Court of Appeal did not exist at this time, so the verdict of one court stood. Even Justice Patterson expected McCabe to receive a free pardon and was disappointed by the home secretary's ruling as he fully believed in McCabe's innocence.

It seems that further enquiries were undertaken by the magistrates in Yorkshire and sent to the Home Office which had a devastating effect on the secretary of state's decision. One part of this new evidence which should, strictly speaking, have been presented during the trial involved the basket that McCabe used for his trade. It seems there was controversy as to whether the basket could be carried on the arm when filled with pots and pans and earthenware as McCabe had stated in his defence. Any further additional damning evidence was not communicated to the public.

The home secretary declared that McCabe was a participant in the crime to a certain extent. He had seen Reid at the door, seen blood on the floor, heard groans in the house, but he neglected to tell anyone his findings, thus making him an accessory after the fact.

The press and the public were scathing against the conduct of Reid's barrister Mr William Digby Seymour who during the last trial understood that his client Reid had made a full confession exonerating McCabe from all guilt. So why, during this trial, did he argue to convince the jury that McCabe alone was the guilty party? Surely, a piece of conduct that must have stamped its author with the utmost detestation for the rest of his life. Some strong accusations and rebuffs were published in the press including the Times newspaper.

Michael McCabe's life was saved, but he was transported out of the country for life. A sentence that today seems unduly harsh, for simply being in the wrong place at the wrong time. Even if he had reported what he had witnessed at the time it was too late to prevent the gruesome murders of three innocent people.

McCabe's punitive and unexpectedly severe sentence had a serious adverse effect on his family. His wife Mary who was described as 'a big strapping Irish woman who refused to work' had a terrible time, she had no money and found life difficult. She lived with her mother Julia Keasley, brother John and her two sons at 97 Upperhead Row and tried to make ends meet on five-shillings a week. She became somewhat of a social problem, so much so that the local magistrate wrote to the Board of Guardians about her, as she was refusing to enter the workhouse and, in their opinion, the woman and her wayward children should all be shipped off to Ireland. A motion was passed to allow relieving officers to take out removal orders for Mrs McCabe and her children, the board said; 'If there were any devils in the world then the two children belonging to Mrs McCabe are it. They are imps! James McCabe uses a crutch, but he can run as fast as a racehorse against any other boy.'

Despite these two boys James and John McCabe being babies when their father was sentenced they were incensed by the treatment their father had received by the English justice system, and had such a bitter animosity towards the police and authorities that they had both joined the 'Irish Small Gang' a notorious group of ruffians terrorising the streets of Huddersfield in the 1860s and had both taken an oath between them to stone the police and cause havoc whenever and wherever they could. John McCabe was the king of this small gang and him; his brother and his mother were constantly in trouble with the police.

Their father Michael was released from penal servitude on 24th December 1862 into the care of the Prisoners Aid Society. He had suffered greatly during his transportation and through illness had found it difficult to work. He died in 1870. His son James died five years later aged twenty-one whilst his other son John lived until the age of fifty-two where he died in Halifax.

This is one of the saddest cases ever to happen in Yorkshire. Not only did three people lose their lives in such a barbaric fashion, but also an innocent man lost his freedom and a family lost their father.

R.I.P.

3

THE ATTEMPTED MURDER BY POISON —
THE BATTLING BELL BROTHERS —
GRINDALE BRIDLINGTON 1856

In April 1856, in the quiet hamlet of Grindale, four miles northwest of Bridlington, a wicker basket was delivered to the train station addressed to farmer Thomas Bell.

Mr Bell had celebrated his birthday that week so when his servant Fanny Wilkinson brought the basket to him, he assumed it was a present. Inside was a stone bottle, which seemed to contain sherry. Mr Bell, feeling in a generous mood, offered a glass to Fanny and other farmworkers named Shepherdson and Hebblethwaite. Half an hour later Fanny Wilkinson was seriously ill and given some dry brandy to ease her sickness. The poor girl was still vomiting the following day.

Despite Thomas Bell only tasting and spitting out a small sip of the amber liquid, the following day he felt ill, his head ached, and he was repeatedly sick. Thomas was suspicious and as it was the weekend, he locked the basket and its contents away. At first light, on Monday morning, Mr Bell took the bottle to surgeon Mr Hutchinson who had a pharmacy practice in Bridlington.

The chemist analysed the contents of the bottle and confirmed that the mixture was laced with a lethal dose of prussic acid. To be sure of his findings he fed some of the mixtures to a cat which died violently, convulsing, and uttering a shrill cry. It seems that the sender's intentions were deadly. The police were informed, and investigations began.

The package was examined and the address label checked, but nobody could confirm the source of the handwriting. Also, the bottle had the name of the supplier on it, which was a local retailer from

Bridlington, 'Kay's of Bridlington' so it was obvious to the police that the culprit knew the area. Investigations revealed that the package had been left at Hunmanby Railway Station late at night, but unfortunately none of the railway staff could recall seeing the wicker basket.

A man named Jacob Tranmer came forward to confirm that he was the person who had left the package at Hunmanby station on the instructions of his master Mr George Bell, the victim's brother. Tranmer told the police that he had left the package at the station at midnight. When he returned to his master's house, he had found all the servants were in bed, but his master was still up, waiting for him to return and for Tranmer to confirm that he had delivered the package as directed by him. Satisfied, George Bell went to bed.

Tranmer told police that a few weeks before, he had bought a stone bottle full of gin from Mrs Kay's grocers in Bridlington. It was lambing season so as part of his job he had to stay up at night and watch the sheep. To keep himself awake he drank the gin a little at a time until it was finished. His master took a liking to the empty bottle and asked if he could have it. He liked it so much that he then sent Tranmer to Kay's to buy two more bottles of sherry. Both these bottles were hidden in the haystack prior to the hamper been sent to the railway station.

Tranmer said that same afternoon George Bell had instructed him to fetch the bottles, and Tranmer had accidentally broken the seal and the contents wasted, but his master filled the other bottle with an amber coloured liquid and put it in the hamper. Tranmer said he had no idea what the liquid was.

The police were suspicious, and to make matters worse Tranmer said that a few days before he left George Bell's employment, the master had offered him fifty pounds, which he increased to one hundred pounds, on the proviso that Tranmer confirmed to anyone who asked that he had taken the basket to the train station of his own accord. Tranmer was apprehensive and soon realised the seriousness of what had been asked of him and refused Bell's request.

This case was deemed serious and a warrant was issued for the arrest of Mr George Bell on the charge of attempting to murder his brother Thomas Bell.

It seems that the motive for George Bell to want his brother dead was based on pure greed and insane jealousy. Thomas Bell had been married for four years, but the couple had no children. His father had owned a farm at Argam not far from Speeton. When he passed away his will favoured his eldest son who benefitted from the profits of this farm, whilst his younger brother struggled to make a living on his own farm at Finley Hill.

In his own will, Thomas Bell stipulated that on his death, if he left no issue then the farm would go to his brother George. At that time property did not pass to the spouse. It seems that George was impatient and needed to get his brother out of the way.

Hoping to catch George Bell unaware, police rode to his farm in Finley Hill in the early hours. Bell and his wife were both in bed, and Mrs Bell objected to the police officer's intrusion into their bedroom, so she asked the officer to wait outside the door while they dressed. The police officer did so, but George Bell was devious, and opened the window, leapt out, and escaped.

In a witness statement, Bell's brother-in-law later stated that Bell had turned up in a distressed state in the early hours of the morning and he had pleaded with him to hide him in the bottom of the gig. The brother-in-law agreed and covered Bell in an apron to avoid detection; they then travelled to a small village called Witherwick then to Hessle where they bought tickets for a passage to America.

America cannot have suited him or maybe he ran out of money, as a few months later he returned to Wakefield, where acting on a tip-off from the public Superintendent Young from Driffield travelled to Wakefield, where he arrested Bell and took him into custody.

Initially, the case was heard before Reverend Blanchard and Mr Reynard at the public rooms at Driffield. An array of witnesses testified against George Bell. One druggist Mr William Smith recalls Bell coming into his shop and bringing in three bottles and asking for one to be filled with prussic acid. The druggist thought Bell was jesting and said 'nonsense, Bell, you're joking,' but realising that he was serious, he warned him against the poison and told him that this stuff was strong enough to euthanize a horse and should not be left lying around the house. The druggist refused to sell Bell the poison.

Thomas Bell took the stand claiming that he had opened the hamper thinking that someone had been kind enough to send him a birthday present. He admitted that he and his brother George had their differences in the past, but Thomas thought that on the day before the incident they had been on good terms. Thomas had even lent his brother some money the day before with no animosity. Thomas Bell did confirm that his brother had a habit of borrowing money from him and at that present time, he owed him four hundred pounds, which he had promised to repay with ten per cent interest.

The defence argued that there was no evidence to implicate their client in any crime. They debated that it couldn't be confirmed that this was, in fact, the same hamper that Tranmer left at the railway station. After all, they argued, the bottle was a common one and could have been left by anyone. Mr Bell had been unsuccessful in obtaining any poison, and it could be that the bottle itself was contaminated and had nothing at all to do with the accused.

In addition, there was no motive for such a crime, after all at the time of the incident the Bell brothers were on good terms. They concluded that all evidence was circumstantial and did not justify a guilty verdict.

The jury retired and after an absence of an hour returned with a 'guilty' verdict with a recommendation of mercy because of the man's wife and family.

In sentencing, his Lordship observed the verdict concluding that he was convinced that morally speaking this crime was no less than murder, and in his opinion, the guilty person had intended to kill his brother. In fact, if the brother had taken the drink then he would be dead without a doubt. While he normally did pay attention to the wishes of the jury, on this occasion he saw no good reason why he should apply leniency in this case. This, he said, was one of the most serious and dreadful cases ever put before the court. Therefore, the judge sentenced George Bell to be transported to the colonies for the rest of his natural life.

4

HUMBUG BILLY — THE LOZENGE POISONINGS BRADFORD — 1858

THE GREAT LOZENGE-MAKER.
A Hint to Paterfamilias.

WiKiCommons Licence

Sweet seller William Hardacre who was known locally as 'Billy Humbug', or 'Humbug Willie' sold confectionary at the Saturday Green Market in the centre of Bradford (in the vicinity of the old Rawson Market and the Arndale centre). Billy bought his sweets from a supplier called Joseph Neal who made them at his premises on Stone Street, close to the Salem Chapel, Manor Row.

On 18ᵗʰ October 1858, Neal needed to make sweets and went to buy the ingredient 'daft' from the druggist Charles Hodgson's shop at Baildon Bridge near Shipley.

At that time sugar was expensive, and 'daft', a powdered limestone and sulphate of lime, was often added in the making of sweets as a cheap substitute. The manufacturer could sell 'peppermint lozenges' for 6-7d per pound, but genuine lozenges which contained sugar could not be sold for less than one shilling per pound.

To make his 'low priced' sweets Neal needed 12lb of 'daft'. Unfortunately, Mr Hodgson was in bed ill, so his assistant, a young man named William Goddard, served Neal that day. Goddard had worked in the shop for only five weeks; he was not an apprentice but an ex-teacher who was helping in Hodgson's shop until an opening became available at the new Inland Revenue Service. Goddard could not find the 'daft' and went to ask Hodgson where he kept it. Hodgson told Goddard that 'he had better not meddle with it!' and to tell Neal to wait until he (Hodgson) was better so he could attend personally to the order. On hearing this message, Neal was insistent that he needed the order there and then. Goddard went back to his master who told the assistant that he could find the 'daft' in a corner of the garret. Regrettably, in this garret were two casks side-by-side one holding 'daft' the other containing arsenic. Neither casks were labelled and the difference not readily recognisable except to the trained eye. The young man measured 12lb as asked. Unfortunately, Goddard chose the wrong cask and the ingredient was measured from the cask holding arsenic.

James Appleton, an experienced sweet maker employed by Neal, made the lozenges. He confirmed that he made the sweets with gum, sugar and mint to make 40lb of lozenges. He also said that he added the 'daft' owing to the low level of the price. The lozenges sold at 2oz for 1.1/2 d. During the preparation Appleton reported that the sweets did not look right, he noticed that they were much darker than usual.

Despite Appleton being ill whilst making the mixture, he did not recognise problems with the ingredients and put his illness down to the start of a cold. It was reported that Billy Hardacre was also not satisfied with the appearance of the dark-coloured lozenges, so much so that he negotiated a discount with Neal, paying 7d per pound instead of 8d. Unknowingly this 'dark' sweet mixture contained as much arsenic in an ounce as would poison a dozen men.

Mistakenly, the damage was done. The sweets were sold in great quantity on the market by John Broadley Edmondson, a yeast dealer who worked for Hardacre on his stall. Five pounds of sweets were sold almost at once, soon after people started feeling ill.

The first fatalities came the next day, Sunday 31st October when two boys aged 9 and 11 were reported dead to the borough police station. Their sudden deaths initially were presumed to be due to cholera, an epidemic in England at that time. The boy's deaths were duly recorded in the 'records' at the station. Initially, there was no cause for alarm as sudden deaths were a regular occurrence in the Victorian society where death and disease went hand in hand.

However, during the day more and more people reported having a sudden and violent illness. The results proved fatal for some 10 people, including some young children, and around 10 times this number within a day or so later showed symptoms of severe illness. The Chief Constable had no doubt that the number of deaths would increase as the days went on. At first, it was thought that a dreadful plague had fallen over the city. The attention of the police officers was driven to find the cause of this sudden and violent, and often fatal epidemic.

One of the police detectives Mr Burniston soon found that the common denominator with these deaths and sudden chronic illnesses was that at some time since 31st October all these people had eaten peppermint lozenges bought from Billy Humbug's stall on the Green Market. The detective visited William Hardacre at his home in North Wing, Bradford and found him ill, and incapacitated. He confirmed that the confectioner Neal made the sweets

Faced with this evidence the police acted quickly and, in an attempt to prevent further harm, Chief Constable Leveratt placed placards all around the town and in the town's beer houses, and all public meeting places asking that if anybody bought any of the sweets from Billy Humbug's stall to return them to the police station. Much excitement followed and over eighty pounds of sweets was recovered from Hardacre himself and considerably more returned from members of the public.

In Jowett Street, two boys, Orlando and John Henry Burran, lay dead and several other family members were suffering from violent sickness. One elderly woman, Sarah Midgley who lived at 7 Margerison Street, Bermondsley (Bradford) had bought some of the sweets and given one to her two-year-old granddaughter who didn't like it and spat the sweet straight out declaring that it 'tasty nasty'. Unfortunately, another of her granddaughters, Elizabeth Mary Midgley, a seven-year-old ate two sweets and was very ill and vomited almost at once. The doctor was called in and the poor girl was doubled up in agony with extreme stomach pains, a burning throat and a constant thirst. The girl died shortly afterwards. The grandmother and her son also suffered from the symptoms of poisoning but survived.

Soon after a further 10 deaths had been reported and 40-50 more people were seriously ill. Chief Constable Leveratt took the decision to arrest Hodgson, his assistant William Goddard and the sweet-maker Mr Neal. They were taken into custody to stand trial at the assizes for the manslaughter of Elizabeth Mary Midgley.

William Hardacre was not fit enough to stand trial as he himself had eaten half a lozenge and was very ill. He was therefore questioned at his own house in the presence of a magistrate.

Felix Marsh Rimmington, a prominent analytical chemist, completed his analysis on the sweets and found that each one of the lozenges had nine grains of arsenic.

Goddard, Hodgson, and Neal were placed in the dock of the borough court. The magistrates present were the Mayor H Brown Esq, Joshua Pollard Esq, WM Murgatroyd Esq and Mr Alderman Rand. The jury listened to the witness and after carefully deliberating on the evidence the coroner summed up his findings. His verdict;

He had no doubt that people had died and many more were ill because of eating poisoned lozenges. It was equally clear that the arsenic had been sold accidentally, that the mixture for the sweets had been mixed up, the intent being 'daft' and not 'arsenic.'

The verdict was that nobody was criminally responsible for the catastrophe owing to the sale of these lozenges. It is perfectly clear that the men responsible were all grossly negligent: Hodgson, Goddard and Neal. However, with Neal, the jury could not understand why he was committed for trial. They considered that there was no *prima facie* case against him, because as far as he thought the ingredient delivered to him by Hodgson was 'daft.' Neal, therefore, had no grounds for suspecting that it would be any other ingredient and especially not arsenic. The jury considered all the circumstances and concluded that in their opinion the fault was with Goddard. However, all charges were dropped against all three men, and what is known as the worst case of accidental poisoning in history was concluded as a dreadful series of errors for which no one was directly to blame.

'Billy Humbug' received a certain amount of sympathy from the press, having been almost paralysed himself. Luckily for him, he went on to continue in business selling confectionery in the Green Market until his death in 1866 aged 61. William Hardacre is buried in an unmarked grave in Undercliffe Cemetery on the edge of Bradford Town centre.

This tragedy and the public outcry that followed were the contributing factors to the Pharmacy Act 1868, which recognised the chemist and the druggist as the custodian and seller of named poisons (medicines). The requirement of labelling all poisons and drugs and the necessity for record-keeping, together with the requirement to obtain the signature and the address of the person wanting to buy any poisons was made compulsory.

Furthermore, the events of the Bradford Poisonings precipitated legislation for the end of wholesale adulteration of food for commercial purposes. This coupled with industrial pressure on the government, led to the development of The Adulteration of Food and Drugs Act 1860, which was later revised in 1872. This Act (1872) made provisions for the appointment of public analysts and regular food inspections controlled by local councils. Two years later the Society of Public Analysts was founded concluding that food should be subject to regular inspections by local authorities.

5

THE TODMORDEN MURDERS — 1868

Illustrated Police News

Miles Weatherhill, a weaver from Todmorden, had fallen deeply in love with a young servant girl named Sarah Bell. Sarah worked as a housemaid at Todmorden's Christ Church parsonage. Her master, Reverend Ploys, was not impressed with Miles and forbade him to visit Sarah. The couple were devastated, and despite the Reverend's misgivings, the relationship continued behind his back. Their secret was not safe for very long as one of the other maids informed her master that the couple were meeting in secret. A disappointed Reverend Ploys ended Sarah's employment. Sarah had no choice but to return to her parents' house in York.

Miles was livid with both the Reverend and the servant girl, and he went to visit Sarah at York. Miles tried to persuade Sarah to return to

Todmorden, but she refused, perhaps Sarah was not as deeply in love with him as he was with her? Sarah gave him half of a necklace she had made from jet, she kept the other half herself as a keepsake.

On his return to Todmorden, Miles' anger had not abated, he blamed the Reverend for keeping the couple apart, and he started to plot his revenge against the master, his wife and the housemaid Jane Smith.

On 2nd March 1868 Mr Ploys had retired to bed when he heard a strange noise at the back door. Fearing a break-in, he tentatively crept downstairs and down the hall to the back of the house where he saw Miles Weatherhill in a violent rage swinging a hatchet around. Seeing the Reverend, Weatherhill snapped and produced a pistol from the back of his pants and fired it. Fortunately, it misfired. Unperturbed, Weatherhill attacked the Reverend with the hatchet. Ploys defended himself grappling with Weatherhill until he staggered back into the house where the noise startled the housemaid, cook, nursemaid and other servants who all rushed to their master's aid pulling Weatherhill off their master by his hair. This allowed the Reverend to escape by the front door, but not before he had received two serious wounds at the back and top of his head, together with some vertical cuts on his forehead, one of his ears was severed and he had deep cuts to both his hands.

The housemaid Jane Smith and the other servants managed to get out of the killer's way by locking the front door, however, an enraged Weatherhill was too quick for them and he put his foot in the back door and gained entry to the house.

Jane Smith managed to hide behind the door of the dining room, keeping her back against the door to keep Weatherhill out. Unfortunately for her he managed to put his hand through the door and discharged his pistol at her. It killed her instantly.

Weatherhill then went into the kitchen where he grabbed a poker and made his way upstairs where he saw Mrs Ploys who had recently given birth. The nurse stopped him at the door and told him that he couldn't go in there. Ignoring her, he pushed her out of the way telling her to mind her own business, as he had already finished those off downstairs. He forced his way past her and into the room where a terrified Mrs Ploys was in bed. Brutally, he tore away the bedclothes and fired a pistol at the petrified woman. Once again, the gun did not fire so he began beating the woman savagely around the head and body with the poker inflicting deep scalp wounds and breaking her nose.

When aiming to strike her again he was grabbed from behind by Mr Stansfield the church organist, who had rushed to the vicarage after hearing Mrs Ploys' screams. Soon after two more men turned up and grabbed Weatherill and marched him to the police station. Weatherill remained calm saying, 'I have done it! I meant to do it, and I am only sorry that the damn pistol (aimed at Rev Ploys) did not go off better.'

The lobby of the house was marked with blood, the house looked like a slaughterhouse. Jane Smith was dead behind the dining-room door.

Mrs Ploys, the daughter of Reverend Molesworth, the vicar of Rochdale, and patron of the incumbents of the parish church at Todmorden was in a state of shock, her husband was seriously injured.

On his way to the police station, Weatherill showed no compassion reaching in his pocket for his pipe.

'I may as well have a smoke now,' he said, 'it will be the last one I will have for I will swing for what I have done.'

One of the men who escorted Weatherill to the police station, Mr Joseph Gledhill, was Weatherhill's ex schoolmaster. Recognising his old teacher, the prisoner said, 'You remember me? I was one of your pupils, you thought I was good with grammar. I bet you didn't think I would end up like this?'

Astonished at his coldness and complete lack of empathy, the dismayed schoolmaster asked his former pupil if he was aware that he had killed the housemaid?

'Aye,' he replied. 'She's got a couple of bullets in her, for there were two in every pistol.'

He went on to say, 'there's no need to hold me, I have no wish to escape. I wish to harm nobody who hasn't harmed me!' At the police station, it was discovered that Weatherhill had carefully planned his revenge, and that his trousers were tied around his waist with a string which had been used to hide his weapons, and that there were four slit holes to conceal the guns. In his pocket were gunpowder, bullets, caps and shot.

He also carried a picture of his sweetheart, who he affectionately called 'his Sarah', he also had in his pocket the part of the jet necklace that Sarah had recently given him.

When the money he had in his pocket was taken out he asked if it could be given to his mother. 'Please tell my mother what has happened, and please tell her as kindly as possible, please say that I shan't be home tonight.' At that time Miles Weatherhill was under the impression that both Mr and Mrs Ploys were also dead.

At the trial, Weatherhill was found guilty of the wilful murder of Jane Smith. When asked how he pleaded he said; 'I did it because Reverend Ploys would not allow me to visit my sweetheart.'

Reverend Ploys died on 12 March 1868 from his injuries, in great pain. Inflammation of the brain had set in and he was delirious. Sadly, the infant child of the Ploys died on the same day as her father. The cause of death was recorded as being due to the unavoidable removal of the child from its mother during the murderous attack on her.

Mrs. Plow didn't live long after the ordeal she had been through. She died at Wantage in Berkshire on the 19th March 1869, just 12 months and two days after seeing her husband and baby daughter buried.

Miles Weatherhill was found guilty of murder at Manchester Assizes on 13th March 1868, before Justice Lush. The convicted murderer stared at the judged unmoved by his sentence. He expected it.

Sarah Bell credit Todmorden Antiquarian Society

Miles Weatherhill Illustrated Police News March 1868

Miles Weatherhill was the last man to be publicly hanged at The New Bailey Prison on 4th April 1868. This prison closed and Strangeways was opened, and executions then took place behind closed doors.

6

THE DEADLY MOTHER — NEWTON-on-OUSE — 1879

Unquestionably, filicide (the murder of a child at the hands of its own parent) is one of the worst types of crimes imaginable. Unfortunately, it is a crime that has occurred throughout the centuries.

In Victorian times illegitimacy was frowned upon and bringing a 'bastard' child into the world did not bode well in the prudish Victorian society. Throughout this era, it would not be unusual to find babies dead or alive dumped in the street, mothers too ashamed to admit their supposed immorality and to avoid the backlash and social stigma they simply abandoned their offspring.

However, this was not the case with the murder of two-year-old John Hammond, who had barbarically met his death at the hands of his own mother in the village of Newton-on-Ouse in York.

Elizabeth Hammond, age thirty, was married to labourer Isaac Hammond. The couple had two children Thomas aged eight and two-year-old John. Although Elizabeth and Isaac had been married quite a few years, it seems that Elizabeth was not happily married, a few years before she had an affair with a man called Smallwood who she loved passionately. Two-year-old John was the result of this illicit affair. Elizabeth fully expected that she and Smallwood would set up home together, but much to Elizabeth's dismay as soon as Smallwood found out she was carrying his child he wanted nothing further to do with her. Luckily for Elizabeth, her husband Isaac agreed to bring the boy up as his own and the couple reconciled.

Still, Elizabeth was not happy and had spent some time in the local poorhouse at Easingwold. As her husband put it 'she had been affected in her mind.' She was there for a few weeks before being released. It appears she was still not well.

Elizabeth was far from being classed as a good mother. She had got herself a job on a farm where she worked long hours and left her children alone all day long with her older son Thomas in charge of his infant brother. Elizabeth or Isaac left no food or drink for the children. One of Hammond's neighbour's said that she often heard the children cry 'Mama drink.'

A few months before the murder, little John had suffered severe burns on his legs and other parts of his lower body. Nobody knew just how this had happened. His father Isaac had gone to Tollerton to fetch Doctor Lantour to see the child. The doctor came the next day. In his testimony, the doctor said that on his visit the mother was out when he called, he said the boy seemed okay. He gave John some medicine and left. Doctor Lantour said the child's injuries had troubled him, so he went back to see the mother, but unfortunately, he could not get to the bottom of how the child became scalded so seriously, as Elizabeth Hammond kept changing her story and always gave a different account of the event.

Isaac said that his wife was with John all the time, and as far as he was aware, she was always kind to the boy.

The night before the murder Isaac confirmed that the last time, he had seen his son the boy was in bed with his mother, both had the bedsheets up to their necks. Isaac thought nothing of it until about 9 pm when the boy turned very poorly. Once again Isaac went for the doctor; the doctor came and gave John some medicine. Isaac did not see his son alive again.

The following morning one of the Hammonds' neighbours, Mary Nelson, who lived close by, called on Mrs Hammond around ten in the morning. She found Elizabeth upstairs and poor little John flushed red in his face laid out in bed on a pillow. The neighbour was shocked and said, 'He's dead…he's dead.' Elizabeth picked her son up by his arms and said, 'Dead he's not dead!'

'Yes, he is dead,' said Mary Nelson, 'It will not stir anymore unless you stir it.'

Another couple of neighbours came forward; Mrs Mary Hughes was going about her business when around 10.45 am there was a knock on the door. When she opened it, she saw Elizabeth Hammond standing there, she said, 'I am glad to come and tell you that Johnny is dead!'

Mrs Mary Ann Tuckman, a widow residing at Beningborough Lodge said that around 11.15 in the morning, Thomas Hammond had called on her saying his brother was dead, the poor lad had tears streaming down his face. He said his mother had sent him, and would she go lay the boy out? When she got to the house, she saw the dead child in his nightshirt. She examined the small child's body and said she did not see anything unusual except the boy's back was unusually dark. She assumed that the boy may have been convulsed. She said that Mrs Hammond was there the whole time, but apart from the other boy, there was nobody else in the house.

Mrs Newton, who lived next door, came to see the child; she said that although she only lived next door, she didn't go in the Hammonds' house often as Mrs Hammond always thought people were stealing from her. Mrs Newton saw the dead boy and said his chest was warm and his feet were cold. She had turned to Mrs Hammond and looked her straight in the eye and said, 'poor little thing, you have often wanted him out of the way, and now he's gone!' To which Elizabeth Hammond replied, 'Yes.'

Hearing the sad news another witness, Mrs Dowson, went to the Hammonds' house, she said to Mrs Hammond, 'Poor thing, have you hurt him?' Elizabeth coldly replied. 'Yes, no doubt I have, he asked me for a drink, so I wet his lips, then I sat on him!'

Shocked, Mrs Dowson then asked Elizabeth, 'how long till the poor boy died?'

'Not long she said, when I thought he was dead I called on Mary Hughes.'

Isaac was sent home urgently from work and found his son dead. He was shocked and comforted by his neighbours. He went to inform the doctor. Once more the same doctor came to the house, he examined the boy finding bruises on his back, his ears were blue and his face was swollen. The doctor refused to issue a death certificate and he suspected that the boy had been suffocated at the hands of his mother. The doctor informed the police of his suspicions.

Police officer William Ambler called at the house where he found Mrs Hammond sat calmly in a chair next to a roaring open fire sewing. He said to her, 'I understand that there is a dead child in the house?'

'Yes, it died Monday last,' Elizabeth replied in a low voice.

She then asked the policeman if he would like to see the child.

The policeman said, 'yes' and inquired if there had been anyone else in the house at the time of the child's death.

'No, I did not want anyone else when it happened!' Elizabeth then took the police officer upstairs, to where the poor boy still lay.

'I want to tell you the truth,' Mrs Hammond said. 'I sat upon the child in bed and killed it, poor thing!'

The policeman looked at the poor boy and noticed a red mark on the right side of his head, ear and neck.

'I did that when I sat on him, this poor boy has gone to rest now. He was not my husband's boy, he belonged to Smallwood, but he didn't want to know. He's been picked on long enough!'

The policeman looked on in astonishment, how could a mother who was supposed to protect her child above anything else, be this cruel and kill him by crushing his body until he could no longer breathe?

As Elizabeth continued with her gruesome confession the events surrounding the boy's death got worse.

'On Saturday night I bought a bottle of laudanum in town and I gave some to the boy. I then gave the empty bottle to my other son Thomas to play with.'

The officer arrested Elizabeth Hammond and took her to Shipton Police Station to await her trial for the murder of her son.

Elizabeth Hammond was tried in her absence at the summer assizes in July 1879. Elizabeth was unable to enter a plea due to her being unfit. She was detained indefinitely at her majesty's pleasure until she was, if ever, able to enter a plea and stand trial.

Poor John Hammond – what a terrible life he had during his two short years.

R.I.P.

7

KATE DOVER — THE QUEEN OF HEELEY, POISONER — SHEFFIELD — 1881

London Road, Heeley

Felicia Dorothea Kate Dover, or 'Kate' as she preferred to be called, was known to locals as 'The Queen of Heeley' on account of her bohemian attitude and fashion-conscious creativity. Twenty-seven-year-old Kate lived with her parents in Thirwell Terrace, Heeley and ran her own small shop on London Road selling confectionery.

A relationship had developed between Kate and an older man, Thomas Skinner, a professional artist who was twenty years Kate's senior. Thomas had started calling into Kate's shop and a romance blossomed from there.

Skinner had been married, but his wife had died suddenly. To help with his daily domesticity Skinner had employed a housekeeper, Mrs Jane Jones, who had also become his business partner. Skinner had devised an ingenious invention, which involved a method of etching designs onto steel. Not only was this discovery revolutionary it had enormous commercial potential. Skinner had spent time training Mrs Jones his trade, and so proficient was she that the couple shared the profits after expenses.

Mrs Jones had recently married and intended to leave her employment once Skinner found a replacement. Kate Dover was introduced to her, but Mrs Jones was unimpressed; she found Kate too flashy and she disagreed with the relationship between her employer and this much younger woman.

Unperturbed by Mrs Jones' rebuff, Kate Dover gave up her shop to become Skinner's new housekeeper. Kate didn't live with him but would walk to his house each morning and returned to her parents' house at ten in the evening chaperoned by one of her parents. The couple enjoyed a good life together, but like many other couples, they had their problems. Both were artistic and both incredibly vain. They argued over money, and Kate's desire to be dressed in the very best fashions. Once, the couple argued angrily over Kate pawning Skinner's goods to fund her shopping sprees. The relationship was volatile, and Skinner was verbally and physically abusive and often raised his hand to Kate.

Despite this, the couple were in love and marriage was planned for February the following year. Kate told a concerned friend who had questioned the age gap between the couple that she would rather be 'an old man's darling, than a young man's slave.'

The day before Skinner's death, friends recall him telling them that he intended to buy Kate a pony. Twenty-four hours later he was dead.

The chain of events started when Kate sent the maid to buy some chloroform and laudanum. Unfortunately, the girl could not provide the required identification, so was not able to buy the poison. Recent lobbying by the pharmaceutical society had pressed for the sale of drugs and poisons to be controlled. Therefore, the Arsenic act of 1851 was introduced, as prior to this the buying of poisons was common and arsenic was used frequently to kill rats and sometimes used as a pigment. It was also used in accidental, sometimes deliberate, and often undetectable deaths.

Kate went to a different chemist with a man by the name of Wood who guaranteed Kate's signature for 'two pennurth' of arsenic. The reason she gave for purchasing the poison was that she intended to use it to colour some artificial flowers, which in December 1881 was not unusual. In this era the buying of poison was commonplace and arsenic and other poisons were used in many instances.

On 6th December 1881, ex-housekeeper Mrs Jones had an abundance of vegetables she had received from a friend in the country. As a gift, she had sent some onions and potatoes to Mr Skinner and Kate Dover. It seems that Kate was not impressed with this act of kindness and hurriedly took the package off Mrs Jones and put them at the head of the cellar.

On the day Skinner died, Kate had cooked a meal of fowl for them both. She had prepared the bird with a sage and onion stuffing, and Skinner asked her if she would also make a separate dish of stuffing with the onions Mrs Jones had sent. Not long after eating some of the meal the couple were doubled up in agony with a burning sensation to their mouths and a heaviness in their stomachs. Thomas' excruciating pain appeared to be far greater than Kate's. Soon after Thomas uttered the words 'She's done for us both this time,' referring to Mrs Jones. Skinner was violently sick, Kate, however, said she felt nauseous and went through the motions of dry heaving, but wasn't sick.

Fortunately, Doctor Harrison lived close by and attended to the couple immediately. The doctor soon realised that despite his best efforts Skinner was very ill; he tried to save him, but he was too late. Skinner died soon after in agonising pain. Doctor Harrison was sure that Skinner had been poisoned. So convinced was he that he kept all the food remnants which, after analysis, revealed that the fowl with the stuffing was clear, but the separate bowl of stuffing made from the onions given by Mrs Jones tested positive.

Richard Skinner was buried on 18th December 1881, at Ecclesall Cemetery. On 23rd. December 1881, an inquest into his death was held at the Victoria Inn, Heeley, before Coroner Wightman. The hearing was held without Kate Dover who was too ill to be taken into custody and she was represented in her absence by a solicitor. According to the local papers she was suffering from hysteria. To make sure she did not think of fleeing the country, two policemen were stationed outside her parents' front door.

At the inquest, there was further evidence against Kate when it came to light that whilst Inspector Bradbury and the doctor were in the house, Kate had hurriedly run upstairs, collected a bundle of papers, and burned them on the fire. Kate admitted that she did this but only because Skinner, whilst dying, had asked her to do it.

It seems that Kate had expected to be the main benefactor in Richard Skinner's will, but she had learned that this was not the case and that her betrothed intended to leave his money and possessions elsewhere. Rumours also suggested that Kate had another sweetheart, and frictions had arisen between the couple, but it was undecided as to whether Kate would go as far as to murder her fiancée.

The trial began on 11th February 1882. The first witness called was Mrs Jane Jones. After formalities, Mrs Jones confirmed that she had married William Jones four years previously and before that she had been housekeeper to the deceased for seven years. She and her husband had continued to live with Mr Skinner after their marriage, and they shared the household expenses. Mrs Jones said that she considered herself a partner in the artist's trade; she knew all the chemicals used in the business and arsenic was not one of them. In fact, she had never seen arsenic in the house at any time.

Mrs Jones confirmed that after she stopped working for Skinner, she remained on friendly terms with him, and that she had no ill-feeling towards Kate Dover whatsoever, and that she certainly denied that she had ever used any type of threat towards the couple and certainly not 'that she would do for both of them.'

Another witness was butcher, George Taylor who had a shop on London Road. Taylor said that he knew Kate and had seen her a few days before Skinner's death. Kate had come into his shop for meat. In conversation, she told him that Skinner was ill. She ordered the meat, and the butcher called at the Skinner house later for the money. Kate said that Skinner wasn't in and that he had gone to the Big Tree Inn at Norton for a few drinks. The butcher saw Kate again the next day and she said that Skinner was always dosing and sleeping and that she was sure that he would soon die. In jest, the butcher replied, 'you will be alright Kate if you got Skinner's money.' He said that Kate had responded immediately, saying that she would rather have him than his money.

Emma Bolsover, the housemaid confirmed that on the day of the murder she had been at the house. She had seen Kate Dover prepare the fowl, stuffing and a Yorkshire Pudding. She had heard the deceased asking impatiently when his dinner would be ready. After his dinner, both Skinner and Dover had become ill. When the doctor called, the housemaid recalled the conversation.

Dr Harrison to Skinner: 'What's the matter with you?'

Skinner: 'I have been poisoned.'

Dr Harrison: 'Hush, hush I will have you right in a few minutes.'

Skinner: 'Attend to her, Doctor, never mind me.' (meaning Kate)

Dr Harrison: 'I will see to her once I have seen to you!'

The housemaid recalled the doctor giving the couple an emetic and afterwards they were both sick. Mr Skinner, she recalled, went upstairs to his room for a lie-down, whilst Kate Dover lay on the sofa in the same room they had dined.

The next witness called was Elizabeth Guest, a domestic servant who lived at 26 Glover Road. She said she had known Kate Dover for about twelve months. She knew that Kate was a housekeeper for Mr Skinner and that he had allowed her ten shillings a week for the household budget, but from this, he expected a quart of beer and a quart of milk each day. Elizabeth Guest recalled Kate Dover telling her that she often found it difficult to make ends meet and that she had to pawn certain things such as Mr Skinner's best suit and a china tea service. Elizabeth said Kate had borrowed money from her on occasions but had always repaid her debt.

The month prior to the death, Elizabeth had seen the couple quarrelling, Kate was crying bitterly and in great distress. Skinner was shouting at Kate and using abusive language. At the end of the argument, Elizabeth saw Mr Skinner throw his arms around Kate's neck and kiss her. Elizabeth heard Kate say to him, 'Oh, Mr Skinner I hope you will forgive me, I will never do it again.'

Skinner replied, 'I will give you one more chance if you will only do differently.'

The couple made up and seemed on good terms. However, two weeks prior to the death Elizabeth remembered the couple having a tremendous fallout. Once again Skinner was shouting abuse at Dover this time yelling, 'You would pawn me if they would only take me in!'

The next time Elizabeth saw the couple was the day of the death when she witnessed Kate and the maid running up the road for a doctor. Elizabeth was concerned and went to see what the matter was. Kate said to her, 'I do not think I will live until the next morning!'

On cross-examination, the prosecution asked Elizabeth if she had seen anything else. She replied she remembered Kate burning a pile of blue papers on the fire.

Kate Dover sat quietly in the court, her demeanour quiet, her face covered in a veil as she listened to the evidence. In her defence her solicitor Mr Lockwood gave evidence.

He said that in his opinion the prisoner had no intention of killing Mr Skinner, that she loved him, and would not hurt him. Furthermore, if she had perpetrated the act at all then it was a case of mischievousness, and only to show her betrothed that Mrs Jones the ex-housekeeper was unfriendly to him; it could be that Kate Dover was jealous of the relationship between them and desired his sole attention. Kate had been perplexed when the onions and potatoes arrived from Mrs Jones, as this to her was a further reminder of the bond between her fiancée and his ex-housekeeper. However, Mr Lockwood stressed that if this was the case then Skinner's death wasn't murder.

He said that Kate Dover was naïve and could have sprinkled a small amount of arsenic on the lunch not aware of the devastating consequences, but he pointed out she had eaten the meal as well. When she saw that Skinner was ill, she did all she could to save him, she had sent for a doctor and even sent for a bottle of lobelia, all acts consistent with her innocence. There was, he said, no willful premeditated murder of Mr Skinner.

With regards to the papers she admits to burning, Kate Dover said that Mr Skinner had asked her to burn them and that she was only obeying his wishes. Lockwood pointed out that if there was a will, and if she was indeed the beneficiary then she had burned the will. Alternatively, if the will favoured Mrs Jones then Kate Dover had provided the name of the solicitor who drew up the will. She offered this information voluntarily, which is another clear note of her innocence.

In summing up, his Lordship said to the jury they had four points to consider.

The first was that there was no doubt that Mr Skinner died from arsenic poisoning.

Secondly, that arsenic was supplied to him in the form of a meal of fowl and stuffing.

Thirdly, that this meal was prepared by the prisoner, Kate Dover.

Fourthly, that Dover put it there with the intention of killing Mr Skinner.

His Lordship briefly dismissed the first two points, saying that the evidence showed that the prisoner had arsenic in her possession and that she had ample opportunity in adding it to the meal that she alone prepared. However, his Lordship argued what was her intention in doing so, what was Kate Dover's motive?

If the jury found that Kate Dover put the arsenic into the meal purposely with the intention of killing Mr Skinner, then they would have to return a verdict of guilty. However, if Dover had put the arsenic in the meal to cause pain, and to put the idea into Mr Skinner's head that Mrs Jones wanted to harm him, and that Dover did this out of an act of jealousy, and that murder was not her intention then the verdict must be manslaughter.

Alternatively, if the jury thought that neither of these two scenarios was on Kate Dover's mind at the time then the prisoner must be acquitted. These were the choices before the jury.

After two hours of deliberation, the gentleman jury returned with a verdict. When asked if they had reached a conclusion the chairman said they had.

They said that they found the prisoner guilty of manslaughter.

A shocked Kate sobbed and almost fainted as she was taken down to the cells, to await her sentence.

The following Wednesday, Kate once again came before the court to hear her plight. She was pale and sobbed all the way through the hearing.

The judge passed his sentence, as Kate stumbled holding onto the rail and had to be held upright by two jurors.

Judge Cave, a celebrated fellow of Lincolns College, who clearly believed that Kate was a murderess passed the sentence of penal servitude for life.

On hearing this Kate passed out and had to be carried out of court to a medical attendant.

A good few years later on December 1895, a petition was put before the Home Secretary for the release of Kate Dover on a ticket. The petition was refused. Four years later her wish was granted; after spending seventeen years in jail, Kate Dover was released on a special licence as a habitual criminal from Aylesbury prison. She was forty-four years old.

Kate Dover died at Rotherham at the age of sixty-nine.

8

THE MURDER OF THE LAYCOCK FAMILY— WHITECROFT — SHEFFIELD — 'OH MY CHILD-MY CHILD.' — 1884

**The house where the murders were committed.
Whitecroft, Sheffield.**

The Laycock family was Joseph Laycock, a hawker, his wife Maria, and four children, Sarah 8, Frank 6, Mary 4, and 2-year-old Joseph. The family lived in a ramshackle area known as No 2 Court off 17 Queens Row, Whitecroft, Sheffield. The family lived in squalor, and the house was in a pitiful condition with one room on the ground floor and two bedrooms upstairs. There was hardly any furniture, except for a three-legged table, a couple of chairs, a cradle, lamp, and a small amount of crockery. The whole house was filthy and had not been thoroughly cleaned in years.

Joseph Laycock had spent all his life in and out of work, first as an errand boy, then as a pot moulder and finally as a hand in a rolling mill. During this time, he had acquired a string of convictions for petty crime, mostly involving theft and drunkenness. He was well known as a violent man – in 1879 he was arrested on suspicion of stabbing a man and had a local reputation as a prizefighter.

Joseph and Maria's marriage was by all accounts, not a happy one. The couple married on May 16th, 1875 at St Phillip's Church, Shalesmoor, Sheffield.

Maria's mother stated at the trial that the marriage was unhappy from the beginning. The couple had frequent rows and were violent to each other.

In June 1884 Joseph spent 21 days in jail for assaulting and beating his wife but the sentence was not a deterrent and within a day of being released there were more rows and disturbances.

According to the neighbours and family, the cause of the violence was the potent combination of jealousy and drink. Maria was a habitual drinker who would fly into violent fits of rage when confronted with the consequences of her drinking. She was, however, a hard-working woman who endeavoured to provide for her children.

Joseph's 'excuse' for his conduct was that he was trying to break his wife's drinking habits but he himself had many convictions and was a repeated drunk himself.

On Saturday evening following his release from prison Joseph and Maria had an almighty row, and Joseph threatened to 'do her'. The following Thursday the couple were seen drinking together in a local public house.

On the day of the murder, there was a terrible violent thunderstorm in Sheffield. Joseph had gone to Banner Cross and witnessed the storm there. His wife Maria spent the morning collecting empty medicine bottles to earn extra money. But after midday, she started drinking. She was accosted in the late afternoon by her mother at The Warm Hearthstone Inn in Townhead Street who accused her of spending money on drink whilst her children were suffering neglect and hunger. On hearing this the landlord refused to serve her and threw her out. Maria was next seen fighting with a woman in Hawley Croft and at 6 o'clock a witness saw her husband Joseph fetching Maria from another pub. This resulted in a street fight between the couple. A policeman walked by and Laycock shouted, 'She's been drinking with another man. Take her in and me an' all.' The police told them to go home at which point Joseph got up and went home to feed the children. Maria, on the other hand, went to her mother's and together with her brother Christopher set off for Glossop Road to sell the medicine bottles they had collected.

On the way back, it rained heavily and so Maria and Christopher stopped at the Bearders public house in Pea Croft for a drink. On leaving, Maria met her husband outside her mother's house and yet another squabble started. This time Maria ran off. However, by 10 o'clock the couple were seen drinking together in The Rawsons Arms in Tenter Street where they consumed some more beer and had supper. They left shortly before 11 o'clock and returned to the house in Whitecroft. A row soon developed but as it was a common occurrence, the neighbours ignored it. At midnight a women's terrifying scream was heard.

The following morning, a neighbour, Ann Kidnew, whose children went to Queen Street school, the same school the Laycock children attended, was concerned that the Laycock house was unusually quiet and that she had seen no movement. Mrs Kidnew went into the house and saw Maria Laycock lying in a pool of blood behind the door, her head was almost severed from her body.

Maria Laycock's body found behind the door

The neighbour gingerly climbed the stairs and saw Joseph Laycock behind the door, his legs moved, and Mrs Kidnew, aware of the man's violence, ran back downstairs without making any further search and ran to another neighbour's house, Mrs Green.

Initially, the neighbours believed that the children were safe and that they had spent the previous evening with their grandmother.

Sergeant Hornsey was called from a nearby police station and he was the first to discover the four dead children. He also saw Joseph Laycock with a gash across his throat. Laycock, barely audible, uttered the words. 'Bob, let me die, don't move me, let me die!'

The sergeant wept when he saw three of the children huddled together next to Laycock. There, at the side of the slain children was a bread knife used in the frenzied attack.

**The bedroom where the slain children were found
Illustrated Police News.**

Joseph Laycock was taken to the hospital. It seems that the self-inflicted wound was administered many hours after the murder of his family. His wound was dressed but was not life-threatening.

The chief constable attended the scene of the bloodshed and ordered that the five bodies be taken to the public mortuary on a corporation dray. Once at the mortuary the bodies were laid out and examined. Maria, apart from the gash to her throat, had cuts and bruises to her face as well as to her wrists, which suggested that she had been beaten and restrained prior to her death. The children all had their throats cut, one so deep that the poor child was nearly decapitated. Another child's thumb was also severed indicating that the child tried to defend itself from the attack.

An Inquest was held the same day by the City Coroner who accepted the formal identification of the bodies and adjourned the proceedings until 1st August 1884. Prior to adjournment, he issued the five burial certificates.

The funeral took place on Monday 14th July 1884. The five coffins were loaded into a mourning coach that had been purchased by public subscription. The cortege made its way along Millsands, Blonk Street,

Furnival Road, Broad Street and Duke Street on its way to Intake Cemetery (City Road Cemetery). Thousands of people lined the route and at the cemetery, there was estimated to be a crowd of thirty-thousand people present. Police had difficulty controlling the crowds as the five bodies were laid to rest in a single grave in the pauper's section of the cemetery. The coffins of the children were carried to their final resting place by their friends.

The inquest was held on 25th July 1884. Laycock had made a statement in hospital confirming that he and he alone, had committed the murders.

He said that he and his wife had gone out drinking. They were both drunk. His wife had shouted to him that 'she wished that she were dead.' At that Joseph said he lost his temper and committed the murders. He said that he first cut the throat of his wife. He then ran upstairs and cut the throats of his three children. He took the youngest child downstairs – a two-year-old boy and sat him on his knee. The poor boy pleaded with his father, 'don't do it to me, Dada.' The heartfelt plea fell on deaf ears, as Laycock cut the boy's throat, then later he said he wanted to die and cut his own throat.

Laycock looked very weak and pale at the trial. As soon as he entered the room, he saw his dead wife's mother. He threw himself into the chair and covered his face with his handkerchief and groaned loudly.

The hearing was held by Mr Wightman, and the first witness to be called was Mrs Jackson, Maria's mother.

'Has tha owt to say to me at all?' she said, looking Laycock straight in the eye.

He didn't and cowardly once again buried his face in his neckerchief. He soon found his voice though and became quite argumentative with some witnesses.

Thirteen-year-old Ada Shaw witnessed that she had seen the couple drinking in her father's pub, the Rawson's Arms. The young girl said she had seen them both drinking at about ten o'clock. Joseph Laycock had three pints of ale; she had asked Maria if she wanted a drink, but she had refused. Ada said she heard Laycock say to his wife.

'You may as well get drunk tonight while you have the chance.'

Maria had replied, 'I don't want to, I tell you.'

Joseph Laycock was not happy with this statement and jumped to his feet angrily interrupting the witness.

'She doesn't know anything about it! She was only there a few minutes. She only served me with one pint of ale.'

Ada was unperturbed and continued her statement saying that the couple had a few beers but were both reasonably sober.

Once again, Laycock interrupted. 'Stupid asking her anything, she knows nowt about it!'

Next to be called was a neighbour Joseph Wright, a labourer who lived at 26 Whitecroft. He said that he had heard Laycock walking up and down the passage and that he knew it was him as he recognised the sound of his heel plates on his boots. Laycock jumped up in anger shouting at the witness.

'You eternal liar, you story-teller you have never spoken to me in your life!'

Next to be called was Ann Kidnew, who confirmed that she knew the Laycock's and that they were neighbours. She said she had seen the children sitting on the step on the night of the murder. She confirmed that she had heard the couple return from the pub and heard Laycock put the shutters up just before midnight. The next she heard was a woman's scream. She went on to describe how she had discovered the body of Mrs Laycock, and how devastated she was on finding out that all the children had been murdered.

Instead of keeping quiet, once again Laycock interrupted the witness.

'If you know me so well you will know that I was in prison for twenty-one days. I bet my missus had another man in the house when I was away?'

'No, I have never seen another man in your house.'

'Seeing as you say you know me so well; what sort of father was I to my children?'

'From what I saw you were kind to the children. I never saw you ill-use them.'

'Have you ever seen my wife drunk?'

'I have seen her drink, but not drunk.'

'Have you seen her with a prostitute called Ellen Cudmore?'

'No.'

'So, you were not outside your house when I chased Ellen Cudmore up the street?'

'No.'

Tom Pearson, who had a shop nearby said that hearing the commotion he ran into the Laycock's house. He recalled the terrible sight. He saw Laycock lying on a mattress. Shocked, Pearson had said. 'Good God, what have you done!' Laycock just put his head in his hands and cried.

The witness said he saw the daughter Sarah, whose head was almost cut from her body. A horrifying experience, he said.

The court was reasonably full, but surprisingly the trial had not attracted the same level of notoriety as some other high-profile cases.

The trial lasted about four hours. During this time Laycock was extremely agitated. When brought into the dock he looked around in an abstracted manner, gripping hold of the rail to steady himself. When asked if he was guilty, he said, 'I don't know, sir!' and burst out crying. He sank back in the chair and sobbed uncontrollably. The court attendants had to console him. Laycock muttered several times. 'Lord have mercy on me.'

When the judge read out the names of his children Laycock sobbed, 'Oh my child, my child.' He did eventually calm down and sat still with his head in his hands.

In his defence, he was described as a thirty-four-year-old man, who was powerfully built with a large head, and his face showed signs of great mental suffering. The defence said that there was insanity in the family and that his father had drowned. Counsel said that at the time he committed the murders he was not in his right mind. However, no member of Laycock's family had been confined to a lunatic asylum.

The jury retired and returned twenty minutes later with their verdict.

'Guilty.'

Laycock offered no response.

The judge said, 'Mr Laycock, I will not add to the misery of your situation. It is my duty to pass onto you the sentence of the law, and that sentence is that you will be taken to the place from whence you came, and from there you will be taken to a place of execution, where you will be hanged from the neck until you are dead. You will then be buried in the confines of the prison where you reside. May God have mercy on your soul.'

Hearing the sentence Laycock's whole frame shook. He gripped onto the rail and looked at the judge in a stupefied manner. 'Thank you, your worship, thank you.' He turned to the police officers and said, 'I have got my doom, this is all I craved for till the judgement day.'

Joseph Laycock was executed on 26th August 1884, at eight o'clock in the morning at Armley Jail. Laycock was the first man to be hanged by Billington, an ex-collier and barber from Farnworth.

R.I.P Maria, Sarah, Frank, Mary and Joseph. You all deserved better.

9

THE MURDER AND MUTILATION OF JOHN GILL — BRADFORD — 1889

Illustrated Police News, 5th January 1889. Copyright the British Library Board.

At twenty minutes to seven on Thursday 27th December 1888, Mary Anne Gill watched milkman William Barrett lead his horse and cart down the street, her seven-year-old son John ran from the house and climbed into the cart, ready to help the milkman on his round as he had done many times before. Little did Mary Ann know that as she waved her child goodbye this would be the last time; she would see him alive.

John Gill was two months away from his eighth birthday in February. A friendly boy who was popular at school and considered to be smart, bright and intelligent beyond his years. He was the youngest in the family with two sisters Ruth and Jane and a brother Samuel.

John was last seen by the milkman Barrett who said John wanted to go home for his breakfast and as he left, Barrett watched him sliding on ice along the road near Walmer Villas, Manningham. At that time Manningham and Walmer Villas was a fashionable and affluent area of Bradford and Manningham was the principal district of the town and home to the town's wealthy people including mill-owners and doctors.

John Gill's father, a cab driver, he was well-liked and respected in the close-knit community. His mother Mary Anne was a homemaker who loved her family. The family lived at 41 Thorncliffe Road, Manningham, then a thoroughfare running from Manningham Lane to the Midland Railway.

When he disappeared, John had on a navy-blue topcoat, which had distinctive brass buttons, a midshipman's hat, plaid knickerbockers, red and white stocking socks and laced up boots. He was of average size for his age with a fair complexion.

When John did not come home for his morning meal Mary Anne was worried, she knew that her son had gone off to help the milkman and that he was on friendly terms with William Barrett and he often went with him to fetch milk from the railway station. She asked around the neighbours, but to no avail, nobody had seen him. Independent witnesses confirmed that they had seen John with Barrett at the railway station and had seen him delivering milk to customers. Barrett himself confirmed that John was with him delivering milk right up to the second to last delivery, but when they reached Walmer Villas, John jumped off the cart and told Barrett that he was going home to get his breakfast. This was something John had not done before; he always finished the round. John never arrived home and was not seen alive again.

Two days passed, and despite the parents putting posters up around the area, and placing an announcement in the local paper, saying 'Lost Boy, last seen 8.30 near Walmer Villas Manningham – Resides at 41 Thorncliffe Road', nobody had seen him since the day he allegedly jumped down from the milkman's cart – there was no trace of him. The days passed, but sadly, John did not return home. William Barrett called on the Gills enquiring if their son had returned? Thomas Gill replied, 'No, I have been to the Town Hall and the detectives are looking out for him, they will want to see you.'

On Saturday, 29th December 1888 eighteen-year-old Joseph Bucke, who was employed as a stableman for Mr Berwick, a butcher who rented certain outbuildings in Back Mellor Street, near where the Gills lived, made a gruesome discovery.

Some yards down Back Mellor Street on the right-hand side going from Thorncliffe Road was an entry about 10ft wide by 15 ft deep, at the extremity of which was a large coach house with large wooden doors. The buildings on each side of the coach house were stables, those to the right were used by Mr Berwick. It was not quite daylight when Bucke arrived at his employer's stable, he began his day's work as he always did by clearing out the manure and throwing it into a purpose made tank on the other side of the entry. When doing so he noticed something bulky lying close to the left-hand side of the coach house. At first, the young lad thought it was a bundle of old clothes which somebody had thrown away. He looked closer and thought his suspicions correct as he saw a boy's overcoat on top of the package. He lifted a corner of the package and was horrified to find a human leg, then what appeared to be a severed ear, and finally, after removing the overcoat, the torso of a child's body, terribly and despicably mutilated.

A shocked Bucke ran into nearby Manningham Lane and raised the alarm. Very soon the yard was full of people. The features on the body were soon recognised of those of John Gill. Mr and Mrs Gill were quickly informed of their son's fate. News of the tragedy spread like wildfire, and people flocked to the area in scores. Chief Constable Withers took control of the scene although the hullaballoo continued for some time. The excitement continued, so much so that once the poor boy's body had been transferred to the mortuary an extra police force was employed to keep the crowds in order.

Before the body was removed, police surgeon, Mr Lodge was summoned to the scene where he examined the body and photographed the remains and the surrounding area where the body was dumped. It happened that the poor boy's legs had been severed from his body at his thighs. His face and throat were untouched, but both ears were sliced off, and a deep vertical cut ran just below the chin to the abdomen. On the left breast were two deep stab wounds. A part of the intestines and the heart had been removed and placed around the neck, and his genitals had been removed. The boy's trousers and shirt were placed amongst the remains which were all held together with braces.

On closer examination, it was discovered that the boy had not been murdered in the spot where his body was found but had most likely been killed and mutilated elsewhere and then carried to the yard where he was found. There were no traces of blood; even the ground where the body was found had no traces of discolouration, a clear sign that John had been dead sometime before he was placed in the shadow of the coach house.

It was proven that the body must have been placed there between 4.30 and 7.30 in the morning. The police constable on duty on Back Mellor Street, Constable Arthur Kirk, said he tried the doors of the coach house on his rounds around 10.30 and they were most definitely locked, and he had even shone his lamp into the corners of the stable and saw nothing. He also confirmed that he had stood on the very spot where the remains were found, there had been nothing there previously. Furthermore, workers from the various mills in the vicinity started work around 5 am, so somebody carrying a bundle would not go unnoticed.

The post-mortem revealed that the boy's lung, which was originally presumed was missing had been thrust into the opening of the boy's stomach. It was also proved that the boy suffered severe fright before he was stabbed through the heart.

At the time that John Gill was murdered the so-called 'Ripper' was terrifying Whitechapel in London. A couple of months before this horrific murder a young girl named Maria Coroner had been found guilty by the Bradford Magistrates and held on a charge of inciting a breach of the peace and bound over for six-months for sending letters to the police and the local press signed 'Jack the Ripper.'

The assumption amongst the police was that whoever murdered John Gill wanted the police and the public to assume that the notorious vicious slayer had travelled north and was now butchering people in the cities. However, it was widely accepted throughout the police force that the murderer was not a stranger within the community, and all enquiries were based on this premise.

Furthermore, a Bradford correspondent reported that a divisional surgeon named Dr Phillips had been to Bradford from Whitechapel to consult with Dr Lodge. The two medical officers examined the body and reached the conclusion that the boy's murderer was not the same man who was terrifying and murdering people in the East End. They did both agree that with regards to the mutilation of the body, that the boy was most probably raped before or after death.

Police called in the services of local Bradford chemist, Feliz Marsh Rimmington to aid with the investigation. Rimmington had opened his first chemist shop in the city around 1842, was well-respected and excellent in his field, and had helped the police with earlier investigations.

Rimmington examined microscopic fibres found at the crime scene. He then inspected the area including drains and sewers. A bloody gag had been found at the scene, which no doubt was used to stifle the poor boy's screams. John also had the remnants of a currant bun in his stomach, which could possibly have been the reason why John was tempted to go 'off' with somebody he possibly didn't know.

The cause of death was given as wounds to the chest. Interestingly, John's clothes were intact and had not been 'cut' through therefore the fatal wounds must have been given in a quiet place when the boy had his clothes off. Strangely, it happened that John's body was drained of blood, and had been washed inside and out, then allowed to drain. Part of the body had been wrapped in a Liverpool newspaper which bore the name 'W Mason, Derby Road, Liverpool' written on it. W Mason was never traced.

The day after the body was found William Barrett was arrested. The evidence against him was circumstantial, but the Chief Constable was not happy with some of the answers and explanations Barrett gave and he demanded further investigations. The evidence was that the boy had not been seen since he was alleged to have left him on the milk-round. A bread knife was found at his house whose blade matched the wounds found on the body. Furthermore, Barrett's stables had been thoroughly cleaned with water and, between six-thirty and the time the body was found Barrett had ample time to move the body to the entry, and then carry on with his usual duties.

Unsurprisingly, Barrett strenuously denied the allegations against him. The bread knife referred to had an 8-inch-long blade which was 1.5 inches in width, with an unusual curvature at the tip. It was clear to the police that this knife had been used for other uses as well as for cutting bread. It also appeared that this knife had been hastily cleaned, but not thoroughly as it still had some dark stains on the point, which raised police suspicions.

Also, a piece of packing material was found by police in Barrett's stable which also had dark stains on it. In explanation, Barrett said that this was used as a cloth for the horses and had become discoloured when it fell off a horse's back to the floor of the stable. Barrett remained in custody, pending further enquiries.

Twenty-three-year-old William Barrett was not from Bradford but from Kidwick, a village outside Keighley. He was very popular in his hometown and had many supporters who believed in his innocence. Prior to moving to Bradford, he worked for the same employer, Mr Wolfenden, who in addition to the Bradford milk dairy owned a farm in Kidwick. Mr John Procter Wolfenden was so insistent of his employee's good character and of Barrett's innocence, honesty and integrity that he employed the services of Mr JW Craven, a well-respected solicitor from Keighley, to defend the allegations against him.

During the police investigations, it transpired that the boy had been stripped naked during the assault, however, all John's clothes were recovered in their entirety. Strangely, the hat was the only item of clothing that had any blood on it. A press representative visited the Barrett house and spoke to Mrs Barrett who was calm and collected and said, 'I have no doubt that my husband is innocent. Regarding the bread knife, the police came to my house and asked to look at my cutlery. I agreed. The constable looked at the knives and took one away.' She affirmed that the knives, along with the rest of the cutlery, were cleaned regularly.

Opposite the entry where the remains were found was a cottage tenanted by an old man named Dodsworth and his son. A light was seen on in this cottage all of Friday evening. Rumour was rampant that the house was a haunt for undesirable characters, one of which could have had something to do with the murder. Police investigated and found that Mr Dodsworth was an invalid who lived in the cottage with his son and that he left the light on for his convenience. Mr Dodsworth said that he had not slept much the night of the murder, but at no time did he hear or see anything unusual. The old man's evidence was vital and shows that the killer's movements were rapid and almost cat-like.

In further evidence one of the Gills' neighbour's, Mrs Kershaw, made the statement.

'I was out this morning about eight-thirty when I met a cabman coming out of Whitaker's yard. He said, have you found him yet? I replied No. The cabbie then said I think they have found a body. I asked if he was dead. He said Yes. I then went around to Mr and Mrs Gills' house and the daughter answered the door. I asked her to go fetch her father. When he came downstairs, I told Mr Gill that they had found a body and that it wasn't good news. I then went away, but I understand that it was the couple's son who told the mother. I am a good friend of the Gills and I was with them until five o'clock the previous morning, as the parents were in a great state of anxiety. The lad was a great friend of the milkman Barret he often helped him on his rounds. He was a good kid and was much loved by his family.'

The Gills' thirteen-year-old daughter Ruth confirmed that on the day her brother's body was discovered she was going to work when she saw a crowd gathered in Mellor Street. 'So large was the crowd that it spilt out onto Thorncliffe Road. I asked a friend if she knew what was going on. She said she didn't. I asked somebody else and they said, "it's John, he's been found murdered.' I was so upset so I asked someone else. They said, no it wasn't him, it was a boy around eighteen-years-old, I was so relieved to hear that it wasn't our John, so I went to work, but I soon came home again when I found out for certain that it was my brother that had been found murdered.'

Twenty-three-year-old William Barrett was arrested the day after John's body was discovered. At 4 o'clock the following Thursday crowds gathered outside the Town Hall when Barrett was brought before the magistrates charged with the wilful murder of John Gill. The magistrates on the bench were Mr Arthur Briggs, Mr James Burnley and Mr John Cass. Only the interested parties were present at the hearing.

William Barrett did not appear to be distressed about the proceedings, whereas Mr and Mrs Gill, who were called as witnesses, were both showing signs of great anguish. On this occasion, Barrett was remanded in custody for a further seven days.

The following week Barrett once again found himself in the dock. This time the Town Hall was crowded inside and out. People flocked to catch a glimpse of this 'Northern Jack the Ripper'. Mr JR Armitage presided, and there was a full bench of magistrates. The case for the prosecution was conducted by the Chief Constable of the borough, Mr Withers, and Mr JW Craven appeared for the accused, while Mr James Freeman appeared for the interest of the dead boy's family.

Throughout the five-hour hearing, William Barrett paid close attention to the statements made, often grasping the iron bars in front of him and turning his head against them so as not to mishear anything.

The Chief Constable said that the circumstances of this case were most unusual stating that the prisoner was a milkman employed by Mr Wolfenden a dairyman at the Ashfield Dairy at 200 Manningham Lane. Barrett's duties were to take a horse and cart from the stable on the back of Belle Vue to the dairy on Manningham Lane and to the railway station to receive milk. He was also expected to work late some nights making butter for the market. The deceased boy lived within 40-50 yards of the dairy. The boy and Barrett had become good friends, and young John often helped with the milk-round.

On entering the court Barrett's demeanour concerned the magistrates; he had his hands in his pockets and leaned carelessly against the rail of the dock. He glanced casually around the courtroom before concentrating his attention on Mr Withers who arose to open the case for the prosecution. The murder of this boy was horrendous, and what's more this young lad was supposedly a friend of the prisoner, yet Barrett showed no emotion and came across as cold and callous. Chief Constable Withers was concerned and wondered if Barrett was insane, he decided to send some officers to interview his family to see if there was a history of insanity amongst them, he also sent some officers undercover to see if they could show if Barrett had a penchant for young boys.

So, if Barrett was guilty of such a terrible crime what was his motive?

The police constable having recapitulated the main features of the case prepared to call witnesses. Alice Peal, a cook employed opposite Walmer Villas, who said that she had seen John on the milk cart when the milk was delivered to numbers 9 and 13, but she had gone away before the cart left so she could not be certain if John was still on the cart or not. Another witness, Nellie Pearson, a single woman, said she had also seen the boy delivering milk to her house shortly before ten in the morning, and seen the prisoner leaning against his cart.

One of the peculiarities of the case is that in all the times that John had helped on the round he never went home early for his breakfast, yet he had on this occasion? Why was this?

Benjamin Abbott, who lived at 125, Manningham Lane, came forward to give evidence that he had been working late at his shop. On his way home, he passed the stables and found that there was a light on, which he said was most unusual. Another witness, Eliza Laird Kendall, the matron from the servants' home at Belle Vue, which is at the back of the stable, was awakened on the Friday night in question by some unusual noises that frightened her as she thought it was someone trying to break into the house. She said it sounded like something scraping and swilling and going backwards and forwards.

She listened attentively but was too scared to look out of the window. She listened until she heard the stable door close, followed by a quick step-down Belle Vue to Manningham Lane. Relieved that the noise had stopped, she went back to sleep.

Lizzie Jefferson, a servant from the Servants Home said she had also seen a light on in the stables belonging to Mr Wolfenden, and that she had seen John Gill there on many occasions, and lots of other young boys too.

Thomas Gill also gave evidence that Barrett had come to his house to enquire after John, however, he thought it strange that Barrett had come in the opposite direction going towards his own home, and not his work. He found that odd at the time. Another peculiarity was that Barrett would have to pass within 40 yards of where the body had been found.

A woman came forward with a very important piece of information which strengthened the case against Barrett. The woman said that on Saturday, the day that the boy's body was found, she left her home at 6.15 and walked down Thorncliffe Road towards Bolton Woods. On her way there she had to pass Manningham Lane. About 100 yards towards Thorncliffe Road she noticed a man carrying a package with both hands, which in her opinion looked like a suit of clothes, but larger. The man was walking slowly and at one time she was almost abreast of him. The man turned down Thorncliffe Road, and she followed him. Crossing over the opposite side of the road she passed him about 10 yards down the road at a point not more than 20 yards from Back Mellor Street where the body was found He continued walking, carrying the bundle in the same manner. The woman turned around and took a good look at the man. At that time the woman had not seen the prisoner William Barrett, but she would be called upon soon to identify him. She had, however, given the police a full description, which fitted that of the accused. The woman was adamant that her statement was correct.

Illustrated Police News.

Barrett's next-door neighbour, Louisa Lenley, said she saw the prisoner leave his house at 5.30 in the morning and walk up Thorncliffe road and then towards Belle Vue where his stables were situated. She confirmed this as this was the time, she reached her work at the mill. Elizabeth Cragg of Bateman Street said that the prisoner had left milk on her doorstep around 10.45; she said that Barrett looked cross and he smelt of drink.

The prosecution pointed out that the parcel – the boys remains – proved that it could not have been carried far, and the fact that all the clothes being removed showed that he must have been killed in some building, and not in the street. Once more the police affirmed that the stables used by Mr Barrett had been meticulously cleaned with water.

Another witness, John Thomas, a dyer and a member of the Salvation Army said that he had also seen Barrett on the Saturday after Christmas coming out of the Belle Vue stable carrying a parcel, which seemed to be very heavy. He spoke to Barrett, but he ignored him, hung his head, and walked on towards Manningham Lane.

The case against Barrett came to a head on 12th January 1889. After hearing the testimony of several witnesses, it was concluded that a prima facie case could not be concluded against him, and he was released to a roar of applause from those gathered in the courtroom.

Barrett seemed unmoved by his sudden acquittal. He was taken down to the cells where he was met by his two brothers Thomas and Fred, his employer Mr Wolfenden and his solicitor, Mr JW Craven and some other friends. The news of his release quickly spread, and a huge crowd soon gathered outside the Town Hall. All eyes were on the entrances hoping for a glimpse of Barrett. The Police thought it very unwise for Barrett to leave at that time, so he waited until it was safe to do so, then he left with Mr Wolfenden and his brother Fred while as a decoy the others in his party left by another entrance and were met by an eager crowd. Some spectators predicted this and were waiting for Barrett who made a run out of the Manningham entrance of the Town Hall and ran to a waiting car on the corner of Bridge Street and Market Street.

As he drove through the streets of Bradford people stared into the car recognising him and wishing him all the best. He went to his employer's house where again crowds of well-wishers greeted him cordially.

Barrett then caught the train to Cononley where his wife had been staying with her mother. A large demonstration was arranged in his favour at Crosshills near Skipton. A wagonette holding Barrett and his family together with the Revered FD Whittaker, vicar of Cononley, was met by the Farnhill brass band playing: 'See the conquering hero comes.' The horses were taken from the vehicle which was drawn up Crosshills by a body of men while hundreds of people lined the streets.

Reverend Whittaker spoke about a meeting he had with Barrett when he was in the cells. He had said to him, 'Look, Barrett, this is a very serious crime, what do you know about it?' to which Barrett looked him straight in the face and replied

'I knaw nowt abhat it!'

At that point, the vicar affirmed that he would stake his life that Barrett was innocent. He went on to say that the prosecution's case was paltry, mean and discreditable to the Bradford Police. He said it was a downright sin and a shame to have put the Barrett family to the great cost and suffering on such a feeble case. They may just have well had said, because they have their knives cleaned, they must be the Whitechapel murderer!

The general census of opinion was in Barrett's favour, suggesting that the police should not have arrested him when faced with such flimsy evidence, and had the police acted with less precipitation then the police could have been on the track of the real murderer.

Illustrated Police News

However, this triumph was short-lived as on the 5th February 1889, a Coroner's Jury sitting at Bradford Court returned a verdict of wilful murder with regards to the death of John Gill. Barrett was re-arrested at Cononley much to the dismay of his family, friends and supporters. Barrett was brought before the Bradford Coroner and formally committed to Armley Gaol to await his trial at the assizes.

At Leeds Assizes on 12th March the Grand Jury did not consider that there was any case to go to trial. A 'No Bill' was issued and Barrett was discharged. Once more Barrett's family and supporters were elated.

To this day the murder of John Gill is still unsolved. There has been much speculation and theories as to who committed this horrendous and barbaric slaying of such a young boy. There are also many unanswered questions. How did the murderer avoid being covered in blood, or even being discovered covered in blood and move around without causing suspicion? Who at that time had the tools to dismember a body? And why were there no other suspects?

In November 1889 the Revered Whittaker received a letter from a man from Beeston Hill, Leeds offering information about the boy's murder. The reverend interviewed the man who alleged that the murder of John Gill was committed by five boys and that the man could not rest with the guilt of this information. However, he was reluctant to give further details saying that he wanted to trace the murderers himself!

John's poor parents must have suffered tremendously over the loss of their beloved son. His death was surely one that shocked Victorian society to the core, and one of the worst murders ever committed.

John was buried in an oak coffin and interned at Windhill Cemetery, Owlet Road, Bradford. Two Belgian horses drew the carriage and hundreds of people followed it. Police had to hold the crowd back as scuffles arose at the cemetery gates as people grappled to look inside the glass windows of the carriage for a glimpse at the coffin. The inscription on the headstone reads:

In loving memory of
JOHN GILL
The beloved son of
THOMAS and MARY ANN GILL
Of Thorncliffe Road, Manningham
Who was found dead December 29th, 1888
Having met his death at the hands of one who
Will someday seek repentance,
In his 8th year.

"Suffer little children, to come unto me
And forbid them not, for of such
Is the Kingdom of Heaven.

Mr and Mrs Gill moved from Thorncliffe Road but remained in Bradford. Thomas Gill died on November 1908, and Mary lived until June 1932. They are both buried with their son in the family grave at Windhill Cemetery, Owlet Road, Bradford.

R.I.P

10

A SCANDALOUS WOMAN — THE MURDER OF MARIA STONEHOUSE — FILEY 1894

Queen Street, Filey

Maria Proctor was born in Muston in 1848; she was the fourth of eight children born to Thomas Proctor and Sarah Edmund. Maria had a twin brother Amos, who died in an industrial accident whilst working for R & B Jacques flour mill in Scarborough in 1870 at the age of twenty-two.

Maria already had an illegitimate son, Thomas William Proctor, when she met Samuel Stonehouse from Scalby. The couple married in 1878 and they rented a seventy-two-acre farm at Low Moor, Hunmanby from Mrs Dale, Scarborough. Samuel and Maria had three more children, Ellen Elizabeth, Samuel Dixon, and Sarah. Ellen Elizabeth died in February 1889 age ten.

By all accounts, Samuel was a quiet, hard-working man, but when he and Maria started drinking, which they often did, their quarrelling and fights were notorious. Both were no strangers to the Bridlington petty sessions and they had appeared before a judge in 1878 on entirely different charges: Samuel (milk-seller) was fined one-pound plus costs for using a horse whilst in an unfit state – the poor horse fell twice whilst attempting to draw a bathing machine out of the sea. Maria (milk-seller) appeared later in the same year for watering milk down by ten per cent and was fined two-pounds plus twelve shillings' costs. This could account for the reasons they moved to Filey, eventually ending up at a small cottage at the end of Barnett's Yard, off Queen Street.

The neighbours were used to Samuel and Maria's drunken arguments and Maria's screams of 'murder' which were often heard when she took a battering off Samuel. Maria did her fair share of the battling and the couple's landlord, John Barnett, referred to Maria as the worst of the two and called her a 'scandalous woman'. Maria could match Samuel when it came to drinking, and many times Samuel would hand most of his wages to Maria on Saturday afternoon, but by Sunday evening, it was all gone.

On Saturday 27th October 1894, Samuel had been working as a bricklayer's labourer erecting new buildings, next to the Spa Saloon. At lunchtime, he called into the Imperial Vaults on Hope Street with friends. Maria soon came looking for him knowing that Samuel had collected his wages; she wanted her share so that she could also go out drinking. Samuel and Maria continued drinking in the pubs of Filey, and Samuel was so inebriated in The Star that the barman refused to serve him any more alcohol. In the meantime, Maria went home to do some baking.

When Samuel eventually went home to Barnett's Yard the fighting started. The couple's two children Sarah and Samuel Dixon were present, and the neighbours took no notice of the throwing of pots and pans – a normal occurrence at the Stonehouse's on a Saturday night. Samuel Dixon was becoming increasingly concerned when he witnessed his father striking his mother across the head with a firebrick. The brick split in two and fractured Maria's skull. Samuel Dixon ran to fetch his uncle Edmund. Edmund and neighbour Amos Danby returned to the house with Sergeant Clarkson, who witnessed Maria lying on the sofa moaning the words, 'Oh my poor body, he has kicked me to death.' Blood was flowing from the wound at the back of her head, and her arm was broken where she had tried to defend herself.

Samuel Stonehouse sat rigid in a chair at the side of the fireplace, his boots were off. He turned to the police officer and said, 'Who sent for you?'

'Your son,' Sergeant Clarkson replied.

Samuel resented this intrusion and became aggressive and yelled at the sergeant.

'Get out, or I will put you out!' he shouted, clapping his hands in the officer's face.

Samuel then turned to his wife and yelled at her, 'Get up – they've come for me.'

Maria did not answer. Samuel turned to the officer, 'She will be all right when she is clear of drink!'

Maria slid off the couch and onto the floor, Danby picked her up and put her back on the couch.

Sergeant Clarkson then arrested Samuel Stonehouse for inflicting bodily harm on his wife and warned him that whatever he said he would repeat in evidence against him. Stonehouse replied, 'I didn't do anything!'

The sergeant took Stonehouse to the police station and when the officer returned to the scene of the crime Dr Orr attended, but it was too late. At age forty-six Maria Stonehouse was dead. The officer took away items of clothing stained with blood for evidence and returned to the police station where he charged Samuel Stonehouse with the murder of his wife. Once again Stonehouse said, 'I didn't do anything!'

There were stains of blood on Samuel's hands and the sergeant drew his attention to this. Due to the severity of the crime, Stonehouse was transferred to Hull Jail.

In November 1894, Samuel Stonehouse stood trial at York Assizes. A post-mortem carried out on Maria revealed that she had a diseased heart and liver, and despite thirty-nine wounds found on her body, the court doctor, Dr Stephens, reported that Maria had died of shock. The couple's children, who were now in the custody of their uncle Edmond, all said that their mother drank.

Samuel Stonehouse entered the dock with a firm step, and when asked what his plea was, he declared, 'Not guilty.'

The couple's daughter Sarah Stonehouse gave evidence to say that before she had gone to the circus field, she had heard her father curse at her mother in Barnett's yard, she also saw him strike her mother in the face. Her mother had then sought refuge at the neighbour's Mrs Gedge's house, but her father followed her. Her mother then left by the front door and then went to Mrs Burr's house. After that, her mother left the Burrs' house and went home to make tea. When Sarah returned home from the circus her mother was dead.

On cross-examination, Sarah said that her father had always been kind to their mother, except when in the drink, when he got angry.

The prosecution addressed the jury and pointed out to them that it was not necessary for them to be convinced that the prisoner hit his wife, this had already been established, also not to spend time deciding if the prisoner intended to kill his wife when he struck her. The intent was there when he caused her grievous bodily harm − the death followed.

The defence argued that Stonehouse had provocation and was aggravated that he did not get his dinner as his wife had been out drinking.

However, the prosecution disagreed saying this was a weak argument and if this was so then why was the prisoner not at home to eat it at the proper time instead of being in a public house? They went on to say how pitiful it was that the couple's children had to give evidence in this case, and that was it not for the drink the father was a kind husband and father. However, on the day in question the row had started by throwing pots and pans, then blow after blow followed before the row got out of control and the deceased had been kicked continually and struck with a brick.

The judge and jury considered this evidence and convicted Samuel of the lesser charge of manslaughter and sentenced him to fourteen years' penal servitude.

The people of Filey thought this sentence was too harsh and they organised a petition. Samuel Stonehouse himself wrote to the Secretary of State to appeal his sentence, all the facts were considered along with the petition and many letters praising Samuel's previously good character, hence his sentence was reduced to twelve years.

When released from prison Samuel returned to his hometown of Scarborough and died in 1920 at the age of seventy-two.

11

THE DOUBLE MURDER ON ROPER MOOR — HELMSLEY 1895 — THE HUDSON FAMILY

Robert Hudson. Illustrated Police News 1895

The inhabitants of the ancient market town of Helmsley, Yorkshire were thrown into a state of great excitement by the discovery on Roper Moor of Mrs Hudson and her one-year-old son Heseltine who had been murdered and their bodies buried on the moors four miles north of the town.

Three weeks earlier, Mr Robert Hudson, his wife Kate – affectionately known as Kitty – and one-year-old son Heseltine visited this beautiful part of North Yorkshire. Robert had been born and brought up in the area. His grandfather, Mr Heseltine, had been a farmer and a judge of livestock on the North Yorkshire Moors. Although he had died in 1878, he was still remembered as a well-respected and popular man and an asset to the local community. Robert's mother died when he was a young boy and his father had remarried and moved with his new wife to Darlington. Robert remained in the area with his grandmother until she died. At the age of thirteen, Robert reluctantly left Yorkshire and moved in with his father, Richard Hudson, at 17 Albion Street, Darlington.

Returning to Helmsley, Robert hoped to convince his wife to fall in love with the beauty of the town and that the isolation and calmness of the moors would persuade her to move to Yorkshire from Nottingham where they now lived. Robert told Kitty that Helmsley was the perfect place to raise their son.

Hudson was described as a steady, sober and industrious man. A cabinet maker by trade, it was while he was working in Sheffield that he had met and fallen in love with Kate Brown the daughter of a wealthy optician in the city. They had married in secret, and once his employers found out, they had sacked him as the company only wanted a single man. Robert was not too concerned as he had inherited money from his mother when he reached the age of twenty-one and he was happy to move around the country, not wanting to stay in one place too long.

In Yorkshire, the family took lodgings with Mrs Mary Anne Holmes on Bondgate, Helmsley. The Hudson's stayed with Mrs Holmes for two weeks, and they were all on good terms.

The Hudson's went on long drives admiring the wonderful scenery and the lovely countryside. Robert tried his best to persuade his wife to fall in love with the area. On the other hand, although Kitty found the area picturesque, she thought it far too quiet and lonely for her.

On 8th June 1895, the family left their lodgings early, but Mr Hudson returned later in the day alone, saying to Mrs Holmes that his wife and child were staying over at Hovingham with his Aunt Ann and Uncle George. He went on to say that they would return on the following Monday and asked Mrs Holmes if she would like to join them on a drive through the moors.

Kitty Hudson and her son did not return as arranged, instead, Mrs Holmes received a note supposedly sent from Mrs Hudson. The note was written in lead pencil asking if Mrs Hudson could pack all her and her son's clothes and send them to her husband's father's house in Darlington. Grudgingly, Mrs Holmes sent all the clothes as requested.

In the meantime, Mr Hudson's father, acting upon a letter he had received from his son, had gone into the local police station saying, that his son's wife had run off with another man and that he couldn't care less about her but how did he and the family go about getting custody of the child?

Hudson had made up a story about his wife leaving him and had written a series of letters to lead his family away from the devastating truth. He had told his father how much he loved his wife and son, and that he had sold all his furniture and would spend all his money and the rest of his life searching for his estranged wife and that he was ready to forgive her – he just wanted her to come home. He had told his wife's sister the same story.

On the following Friday Kitty's sister, Agnes Robinson came to Helmsley from Sheffield with a letter from Mr Hudson saying that his wife had 'gone away' and he regretted to inform her that she had been unfaithful to him and had 'ran off' with a Helmsley man. Agnes was suspicious, she knew her sister well and doubted that she would ever turn her back on her marriage vows and be adulterous to her husband. Furthermore, Kitty would never go out alone, and would not have had the opportunity to be unfaithful even if she wanted to. Agnes was concerned and began to make enquiries.

Kitty's anxious sister soon found that no visit had been made to the family in Hovingham, doubts aroused. Agnes and her family went to see Hudson's parents at Darlington. Agnes asked to see Kitty's clothes but was told that they were all in the wash.

Not convinced, doubts were getting the better of Agnes so she returned to Hemsley with her cousin where she found that, like her, people were suspicious and several people were determined to find the whereabouts of the young woman and her small boy, so a search of the moors was made.

Initially, nothing was found until a gamekeeper named Robert Baker said that whilst looking for the missing people, he came across three men who were also searching. One of the men named Robert Tyerman said he had seen something unusual whilst he had been repairing the road close to the moors and whilst he had sat down to eat his packed lunch on a seat opposite a certain part of the heath, he saw a large hole, which had recently been dug under a clump of trees twelve yards distance from the Moor Road.

On closer examination, he called his workmates and they discovered that this large hole looked like it had recently been dug over; the hole had a stick poking out of the top of it. The men investigated and one of them prodded the ground with a hooked stick and soon came across bone and flesh. The police were called and three inches down they discovered the first body, then the body of a baby, which were later identified as the remains of Mrs Hudson and her son Heseltine.

Both victims had deep cuts across their throats and a large carving knife was found laid across Mrs Hudson's breast. Both bodies were taken to Helmsley mortuary for an inquest where it was found that Mrs Hudson had put up a fierce struggle, as her hand was broken and badly cut. The poor woman had received a bullet to the right side of her head, which had not killed her but had enabled the accused to carry out his deed.

Finding Bodies. Illustrated Police News 1895

Kitty's sister Agnes received the news via telegram, which simply said 'Kitty and the child have been found dead'.

The inquest into the murders was heard at the Feversham Arms in Helmsley conducted by the coroner, Dr Porter. Agnes Robinson had the distressing job of identifying the bodies which could not have been easy as the bodies were both in an advanced state of decomposition.

The Landlady, Mary Anne Holmes, confirmed that when Mr Hudson returned to his lodgings alone, he had said that his wife and son had gone off to visit his aunt. She did note that he looked very agitated and was sweating profusely. She also said that when she had gone upstairs to change the water in the washstand, she had noticed that the water in the bowl was sandy and gritty. However, she confirmed that there was no blood in it. She said that at the time she thought it very strange. Hudson left shortly afterwards, saying he was going to join his family. He returned sometime later to collect his bicycle, again in a disconcerted state.

After hearing various witnesses' statements, the coroner summed up the case. Momentarily the jury returned with a unanimous verdict of willful murder against Robert Hudson. Now all the police needed to do was find him as Hudson had disappeared.

Police were on the alert for the apprehension of Robert Hudson and had circulated his picture across the country. The press was in a frenzy, willing to interview anyone who had the slightest information on this double killer.

On 22nd June 1895, a tip-off came in from Worcestershire police that a man answering Hudson's description had taken lodgings at 75 Dawlish Road, Selly Oak, Birmingham. Police travelled to the house where they found Hudson reading a comic paper. At first, he denied that he was Robert Hudson, saying that his surname was Robertson, but he soon changed his mind. In his rucksack were several pictures of him, his wife and baby, and in his pocket were several cartridges, a revolver was found in his rucksack. He also had a large carving fork which matched the knife found on Kitty Hudson's body.

Hudson was transported by train back to Yorkshire. A large crowd gathered at York railway station to hoot and jeer at Hudson as he passed through the station on his way to Malton. He arrived at Malton handcuffed to Superintendent Silverside and another officer, Inspector Dennis of Kirkbymoorside.

Speculations as to the reason why Hudson would want to kill his wife and baby were widespread, some said that Hudson had grown tired of his wife since the baby was born. That he wanted someone new and had spent some time advertising and replying to notices he had placed in the press for women who were looking for company. When arrested he had a handful of carte-de-visite cards in his possession.

Hudson's parents were overawed and devastated at their son's actions and were at a loss to understand what led him to commit such an appalling crime. They said that as a boy Robert was irreproachable and the last person you would ever suspect of committing a crime and certainly not murder!

They went on to say that so excellent was Robert's disposition that a local clergyman took a great interest in him and wanted Robert to study for the church. Mr and Mrs Hudson said that the church worshipped the ground he walked on. Robert, they said, was the best of sons; a good boy-and a regular churchgoer, a Sunday school teacher and a sensible, sober young man. Mr and Mrs Hudson did not believe that Robert was in his right mind when he committed these horrendous murders.

Richard Hudson said what preyed on his mind was that he believed that his son killed his wife and child as he did not want them to ever want for anything. He did not comprehend the rumours that Robert was actively seeking another woman, although he did admit that he was shocked to discover that Robert had placed adverts in the papers for a suitable wife, which his father said proved just how un-hinged his son's mind was.

He also made the point that his son had ample opportunity to flee the country, but he didn't. Robert had told his father that when on the run he had followed two detectives whilst they were searching for him in the streets of Birmingham.

Mr Hudson said that his son had always shown the greatest affection for his wife and when the couple came to visit people commented that they were more like lovers than a married couple. He and his wife also stated that this 'foul deed' was as much of a mystery to them as it was to anyone else.

The case against Hudson was heard at York Assizes on 24ᵗʰ July 1895 before Judge Matthew. For the prosecution was Mr Waddy QC and Mr Blake, for the defence was Mr Wraggle.

The prosecution argued that Hudson had planned the murder so he could be free to find another woman. Letters alleged to have been written by him to various matrimonial agencies were produced in evidence. Hudson denied that they were his letters. The defence disagreed stating the on the day of the murders Hudson was not in his right mind, that he was of a delicate disposition and suffering from epilepsy at the time. Three doctors examined Hudson, and all found that he was sane at the times of the murders and that he knew perfectly well what he was doing at the time.

The evidence for the prosecution was circumstantial, but it did seem that Hudson didn't try to conceal his movements while in Hemsley. A few days prior to the murders he was seen cycling near the spot where the bodies were found, carrying a shovel. However, he did not return with a shovel which suggests that his actions were premeditated. Witness's confirmed that they had seen Hudson and his wife and child on the moor, but his wife and son were never seen again. Hudson left his lodgings with a feeble account of where his wife and child were heading. Unfortunately, this information was untrue, and their bodies were found shortly after.

Hudson refused to let his family provide any type of defence for him. On the day of the hearing, all eyes were on him as he entered the dock: a smartly dressed young man, good looking with an air of insouciance about him.

There was a silence in the courtroom when the charges were read out to him; once more Hudson showed no sign of emotion.

The clerk to the court asked him how he pleaded. Robert failed to answer. The clerk repeated his question more decisively. Robert answered, 'Not Guilty.'

The jury was sworn in, and the evidence presented to them, describing in full detail the graphic savagery to which both victims were subjected to, and the struggle that Kate must have ensued to save her life and that of her small child. The prosecution also said that there was the possibility that Kate had still been alive when placed in the shallow grave. Her son, however, was not – his throat had been cut almost to the bone.

Furthermore, the prosecution made it clear that they believed that the murders were premeditated. In addition to the evidence of the spade being left on the moors in readiness for Hudson's cruel intentions, the police also found an entry in Hudson's diary exactly one week after the murder that read, 'One week from the saddest ever day of my life; ten minutes to one o'clock and I am still alive.'

Regarding possible motive, it came to light that Mrs Hudson and her son had both been left a considerable sum in the will of a relative (one-hundred and seventy pounds – approximately forty-thousand pounds in today's money 2019). Hudson, it seems, had spent the money his mother had left him and was struggling financially. This, together with the strange adverts for a 'wife' he had placed in the press, all went against him.

The jury was asked to consider the evidence and duly retired to consider their verdict.

Hudson was removed from the dock. Throughout the proceedings, he was calm and did not appear to have the slightest bit of remorse. He did not have to wait long in the holding cell as within ten minutes the jury returned with their verdict.

Once more the court was silent as Hudson was brought back into the dock to hear his fate. All eyes were on him as each of the jurors were asked if they had reached a verdict, they all nodded their heads. 'Do you find the prisoner at the bar, guilty or not guilty?'

The foreman answered in a clear tone. 'Guilty.'

The judge then informed Hudson that he must now accept the law of the land and Hudson was sentenced to death. Hudson accepted the verdict in an unconcerned manner and walked firmly from the dock.

A great crowd gathered in the prison yard all anxious to hear the verdict. A roar of applause soon arose once the result of the trial was conveyed.

Tradition stipulated that three Sunday's must pass before the sentence could be carried out, a custom which apparently existed to give the condemned person a chance to repent on his or her sins. Also, an execution did not usually take place on a Monday, to allow the hangman enough time to travel to his destination.

Whilst in prison, a Yorkshire Post reporter visited Hudson's family at Albion Street, Darlington. His devastated parents were beside themselves, although they were resigned to the inevitable outcome.

Sorrowfully, they told the reporter what a promising life their son once had, showing the reporter pictures of Robert and his siblings, together with a picture of him and Kate on his wedding day.

Deep grief encompassed the family. Their neighbours had been good and rallied around them. Mr Hudson said, 'If it wasn't for the neighbours, we would not have been able to bear up in our troubles.'

Their condemned son corresponded with his family regularly and had shown great empathy, love and affection for them.

However, despite writing to his parents a couple of times a week, he did not admit his guilt, he did though offer expressions, which do in themselves confirm that he was aware of the gravity of his serious situation and that he was filled with regret.

Mr and Mrs Hudson were at a loss to understand just what led their son to commit such a terrible, vile crime. Mrs Hudson, desperate to know the reasons why he did what he did, wrote to her son pleading with him to write to her the day before the execution. He didn't.

Mr and Mrs Hudson, together with their two sons and two daughters visited Robert before his death, then immediately left for a few days break at the seaside to allow them to come to terms with their grief during this exceedingly painful period.

The execution was at York Castle, with Billingham as the executioner who had travelled to York a few days before. The previous evening Hudson retired at ten and slept well until six the following morning. He dressed, had his last breakfast and spent some time with the prison chaplain.

Twenty-three-year-old Robert Hudson walked firmly from the prison to the gallows without changing his countenance. Billingham carried out his instructions, Hudson's death was instantaneous.

R.I.P Kitty and Heseltine.

12

THE HORRIFIC MURDER OF FIVE-YEAR-OLD BARBARA WHITIAN WATERHOUSE —HORSFORTH — 1891

Walter Lewis TURNER

On the morning of the 6th June 1891, five-year-old Barbara Whitian Waterhouse, the daughter of Elizabeth and David Waterhouse, a quarryman from Horsforth, sat and ate her breakfast with her mother and the other members of the family. She appears to have stayed at home, in Alma Yard, Horsforth, until about eleven o'clock in the morning. She then went out to play, and her mother saw nothing more of her. Barbara was spotted in Town Street where she was seen looking into the shop windows of Mr Dean a boot and shoemaker, and Mr

Robert's grocers' shop. Another witness confirmed that she had seen Barbara peering into the window of Mr Pointon's shop on Town Street, Horsforth, from where she disappeared. A police search was started, and local people joined in to look for her, but with no success, the little girl had vanished into thin air.

Five days later Police Constable Moss was undertaking his usual patrol in Leeds town centre, when he approached the corner of Alexander Street, opposite the municipal buildings of the Town Hall and the police station when he came across a bundle. PC Moss, on his usual beat, had not long since checked this area, and the bundle was not there then. Puzzled, he looked inside and was horrified to find the mutilated remains of a female child. The girl's throat had been cut ear-to-ear, her body was ripped open, her intestines laid bare, her arms and legs almost severed from her body. The mutilation of the girl's body bore similarities with the murder of John Gill in Bradford two years earlier. It also resembled the slayings in London by the so-called Jack the Ripper.

Friday 12th June, a fifty-two-year-old woman named Ann Turner, a widow who lived in Horsforth, walked into the detective office at Leeds Police station and made an extraordinary confession. She implicated that her thirty-two-year-old son, Walter Lewis Turner, had murdered the girl the police had found a few days before. Initially, Chief Inspective Sowerby and Detective Sergeant Mackenzie were sceptical, nevertheless, very soon the woman's story held credence. This is what Ann Turner told the officers in her statement.

'I have a son aged 32, a weaver by trade. He works at Lonsdale's mill at Horsforth. On Monday last I noticed a bundle in the coal house under the stairs in my house. It was wrapped in a shawl. I asked my son what was in the bundle. He replied: 'I'll tell you about it sometime. It is nothing I have done!'

Ann Turner confirmed that she did not look inside the bundle, but she had prodded it. 'I knew something was wrong,' she continued, 'as I had used the shawl on my son's bed.' The officers showed Mrs Turner the worn and shabby shawl and she confirmed that it was hers.

Mrs Turner said that on the previous Wednesday evening her and her son Walter had placed the bundle in a yellow tin box and taken the train into Leeds, they had then walked across to the centre of Leeds to her daughter's house, then they eventually left the bundle in the street at the rear of the Town Hall, after that her son walked home, arriving at the house around one o'clock in the morning.

The officers accompanied Mrs Turner to the train station where on the platform was the yellow tin box. The box was tied together with a piece of string. The officers opened the box where they noticed a pungent smell of chloride and lime. The officers spoke to the guard who confirmed that he had seen the couple with the box on the previous Wednesday evening.

Mrs Turner said that she and her son had first taken the box to her daughter and sons-in-law's house Mr and Mrs Joy on Crown Street where they left it. afterwards, they took the bundle to the spot where the body was found. The officers escorted Mrs Turner to Leeds centre where she confirmed the exact place where they had left the bundle.

The officers interviewed Mrs Turner's daughter and at their house in Crown Street, a deaf and dumb couple who later confirmed that they had seen Mrs Joy's mother Ann and her brother Walter Turner on Wednesday evening and that the tin box had been at their house until the Friday afternoon when the Turners came to collect it. The officers were happy that this couple had nothing to do with the murder of this innocent child.

Satisfied with the evidence before them, Chief Superintendent McWilliams and the two officers went to Horsforth and were met at the station by Sergeant Poyser of the West Riding Police force. Together they went to Turner's house, which incidentally was directly opposite Mr Pointon's shop the last place Barbara Waterhouse had been seen alive.

Turner was arrested and all he had to say for himself was: 'You'll have to prove it!'

Officers searched the house where they found stuffed up the chimney a bundle containing children's clothes. Also, blood had been found in nearby Mossley Woods.

Barbara's parents, David and Elizabeth, had arrived at Leeds mortuary to positively identify the body. Mr Waterhouse was asked to do it, as officers thought that the terrible injuries the girl had suffered would be too much for Mrs Waterhouse to bear. Even Mr Waterhouse was only allowed to see his daughter's head and face, and not the poor girl's mutilated body. He was led away crying, 'My poor baby, my poor Barbara.' Mrs Waterhouse was insistent that she should be given the right to see her daughter one last time. As predicted, it was all too much for her; she fainted in the mortuary room and had to be revived.

Dr Ward, the police surgeon based at Leeds Infirmary, carried out the post-mortem and verified that the little girl had been 'subjected to ill-usage' prior to the murder. The girl's clothes had been put on her after her murder as there were no signs of any blood on her clothing. The poor girl had been terribly mutilated. The first wound was in the pit of her abdomen and she had wounds on both her hands proving that the girl must have struggled with the knife when trying to defend herself. According to the medical testimony, the lower part of the unfortunate girl's body was ripped open in such a brutal manner before death ensued. Barbara must have suffered in terrible agony.

Similarities, between this murder and the murder of John Gill in Bradford some years previously came to the attention of the police. By all accounts, a woman had started a rumour that the Turners lived on the same road as the Gill's at the time of John's murder and that Walter Turner was employed as a weaver at Manningham Mills. However, this statement bore no truth. Turner did not live in Manningham at any time and had never been employed at Manningham Mills. Walter had an alibi at the time of the boy's murder – he was with friends in Leeds, who all confirmed his story.

The police also received an anonymous letter saying to ask Turner about Bradford, and if the police charged him with Johnny Gill's murder Turner wouldn't deny it. The letter also told them to ask him about the attempted murder of his wife when he had cut her throat leaving her for dead!

The allegation about his wife was true, the inhabitants of Shipley knew Turner's name well. Eighteen months previously Walter had lived there with his wife Ellen, a respectable woman and the daughter of Mr Oliver Hainsworth of Titus Street, Saltaire. The couple lived together at 17, Thompson Street, Shipley. Turner was employed as a weaver at Saltaire Mills. The couple lived together reasonably well except for Walter's drunken and dissolute behaviour. Eventually, the couple separated. But they reconciled some months later, which was going quite well until Turner relapsed into his old drunken habits.

Saturday 17th August 1889, Turner came home drunk and had a row with his wife, by all accounts he had been drinking all week, and his wife had had enough and refused to go up to bed, choosing instead to sleep downstairs in a chair all night. The following morning, Ellen awakened to a feeling of something sharp at her throat. She looked up and saw her husband standing over her with a razor in his hand. She struggled with him and knocked the knife out of his hand. He briefly came to his senses shouting, 'Oh what have I done?'

He got himself dressed and ran from the house. Ellen, feeling blood on her throat, screamed which soon drew the attention of her neighbours who alerted the police. Turner went on the run for a few days but gave himself up at the Leeds Assizes and received a sentence of nine months' imprisonment.

This was the last straw for his wife Ellen Turner, she left the country for America never to return.

Meanwhile, the detectives were working hard on the case. The bedclothes from Turner's bedroom had completely disappeared, all that was left in the room was a bed, mattress and a couple of pillows. The police assumed that the bed sheets must have been removed as they were covered in blood. They interviewed Mrs Turner again, and a clearer picture of what happened that terrible day began to appear.

The day after Barbara went missing Mrs Turner had her twelve-year-old grandson, George Holder Joy, over to stay. The grandson slept in the same back bedroom as his uncle Walter Lewis Turner, but it seems there were no bedclothes on the bed where the boy slept. The police were curious. It appears that although there was a bed in the room neither Turner or his nephew slept in it, they both apparently slept on a mattress on the floor covered with Turner's overcoat.

Mrs Turner gave a statement, saying that on Sunday morning Mrs Turner had got up and said to her son that she was going to light the fire. Walter was most indignant to this, and told his mother aggressively, 'No', that he would do it. When she went into the front room, she saw that her son had moved the sofa up against the cellar door. He then lay on the sofa all day; he was quiet and very sleepy.

The following day, whilst her son was sleeping upstairs, Mrs Turner crept downstairs and pulled the sofa away from the wall, she then went down into the coal cellar and struck a match and saw a bundle in the corner of the room. She said she touched the bundle and a cold shiver went through her body. She screamed and rushed upstairs to get dressed, she intended to go out into the street and tell somebody what she had seen and that she suspected that her son was a murderer, but Walter heard her and hurried from his room. She said that Walter hugged her so tight that she couldn't move. I asked him 'what have you done son?' he replied 'Nothing.'

A friend of Ann Turner, Mrs Cotterill of 91, Portland Crescent, Leeds had known the Turner's for over seventeen years. At the trial she gave evidence saying that Mrs Turner had visited her in great distress, she had said 'In my house, there has been nothing less than murder!' An intuitive Mrs Cotterill had replied, 'Is it about that missing child from Horsforth?' To which Mrs Turner had responded, 'I suppose it is.' Then agitated, she added, 'I am as innocent of it as you are!'

Mrs Cotterill urged her friend to go to the police and to take the body to the Town Hall in Leeds as soon as possible to clear herself, she said that if she didn't tell them then she would. She also said that Ann had told her that Walter kept saying it wasn't him that did it but that it was: 'Jack that done it!'

The trial began at Leeds Assizes on 7th August 1891. Walter Lewis Turner, aged 32, a weaver and his mother was charged with the murder of five-year-old Barbara Waterhouse from Horsforth. Ann Turner was indicted for been an accessory after the fact.

A hum of voices spread around the courtroom as Ann Turner was called to the bar, every neck was craned to see the wretched woman brought into the dock by a female officer. She was taken to the witness box and sworn in amid a breathless silence. No evidence was offered in respect of the capital charge, therefore this charge against her was held over. His Lordship issuing a verdict of 'Not guilty.'

Slowly, in a low but audible voice, Mrs Turner detailed the evidence against her son.

MRS. TURNER.

In summing up, Mr Justice Grantham spoke of Mrs Turner saying, 'she was one of the most unfortunate creatures that had ever breathed. Her only offence was the maternal love for her son, a love that every woman has for her offspring, scared that the police would let loose on him she attempted to shield him. She has not done right, but wrong by aiding and abetting a murderer.' The judge sentenced her to penal servitude for the rest of her natural life.

On Saturday 8th August the trial resumed, once again the courtroom was packed. After hearing all the witnesses the judge summed up the evidence and the jury left to consider their verdict. After only fifteen minutes the jury returned, saying that the jury was unanimous in there decision and that they found the prisoner Walter Lewis Turner guilty on the capital charge.

Asked if he had anything to say, the prisoner asked the judge if he could say a few words.

'I want to assert my innocence, as I have always done and always will do. Many witnesses have testified of my likeness for children, which would prevent me from doing such a terrible crime. I am not guilty!'

The learned judge put on the black cap and addressed the prisoner. 'Walter Lewis Turner you have been very properly found guilty of the most atrocious crime that has ever been my lot to try, and on evidence which could not have left any doubt as to your guilt. It was fortunate that since this horrendous murder you have been under the protection of the law, and now the time has come for you to meet your doom under that law. Had you not been under the protection of the law, then there would have been plenty of people, and no law or no amount of police officers would have been able to stop them tearing you limb from limb. It is not for me to fathom the motives why you found it necessary to commit this revolting barbarity or to discover what fiendish love of blood could have made you commit such an inhuman crime. That I leave to your conscience and your God. The jury has done its justice, now it is time for me to do mine.'

His Lordship then passed a sentence of death in the prescribed form. A loud cheer came from the court.

The prisoner received the sentence with an apparent air of indifference and walked calmly down to the cells below.

After the prisoner had retired to the cell. His Lordship called Mrs Waterhouse, the mother of the murdered child, to him where he presented her with a large bouquet of flowers. On leaving the Town Hall, Mr Justice Grantham was subjected to a most unusual demonstration at the hands of thousands of people, who cheered him vociferously on his driving off in the High Sheriff's carriage.

The following Monday the judge requested Mrs Turner's daughter and her husband, Mr and Mrs Joy and Mrs Cotterill to attend court at one o'clock. Once the parties were gathered the judge said, 'I have sent for you all today to thank you for your conduct in court through what must have been a most distressing time through one of the most horrific murders that has ever come to light. You have all acted in a professional manner, despite knowing the complexities of the crime, yet you acted in a way that reflected the greatest credit to you all.

Unfortunately, one of your relatives did not act in the same way, but by her conduct and her actions did her best to prevent the detection of this crime. Had it not been for your honesty and advice that crime may have remained undetected. For her part in this crime, she deserved a stiff and fitting punishment as a deterrent to others.

'I postponed until today the announcement of the reward I am going to give you. And that reward is the hope of restoration to you.

The mother and friend who by her actions had necessitated such a severe sentence. What better reward can I give you, for your good conduct than that of the life that had practically been taken from you. I have much pleasure, Mrs Joy, to inform you that I have given orders that your mother's sentence is reduced to twelve months imprisonment.'

This news was welcomed with great praise and gratitude from the parties.

The date of the execution of Walter Lewis Turner was set for 8 am on 18th August 1891. In the meantime Turner continued to express his innocence, even writing letters to his solicitor explaining what happened the fateful day that this poor five-year-old girl lost her life in such a horrific way.

He wrote in his letter how he had spent the morning of the 6th June. He had intended to go to work, but he didn't feel like it so he didn't go. Instead, he met his friend Watson who he met whilst he was a patient at Leeds Infirmary. He and Watson went for a drink at the Black Bull Inn. Watson didn't stay too long, but looking out of the pub window he saw his friend Jack. He ran out of the pub to meet him and they then went back to his house where they drank more beer. Turner said that after a few drinks he had felt drowsy and went up to his room to lie down on his bed. When he awoke he felt woozy and went downstairs where, to his horror, he saw the murdered remains of a small girl placed between the doorway and the foot of the staircase. Without thinking he ran upstairs and fetched his mother's shawl, then he wrapped the poor child up in it and put the body in the coal house where his mother later found it. He didn't tell anyone the truth at the time, as he didn't think anyone would believe him, bearing in mind his reputation and that he had recently been released from prison for attempting to murder his wife.

The prison governor simply scanned the letter, he didn't even take a copy of the letter dismissing its content completely. In his opinion, Turner was guilty and deserved all he got.

Armley Gaol 7.45 Tuesday 18th August 1891.

The night had been very wet, the rain had fallen for hours, and every now and then a mist had hung over the town giving everything a dreary aspect. By six-thirty, many people had started to gather at the gaol. The arrival of the officials created interest, but the crowd remained in good order. At every strike of the prison clock mutterings were heard through the crowd as to how long the prisoner had left to live. Billington was to be the executioner. He had arrived the day before and ensured that all the final preparations were in order. A new scaffold house had been erected on the north-east wing of the prison, the exterior of which resembled that of a gentleman's coach house. Furthermore, the place of execution was not more than fifteen yards from the condemned cell. Moreover, Turner did not have any steps to ascend. Near the execution house are various mounds showing where previous murderers have been interned. Turner's grave had already been dug and was nine-feet deep.

The chaplain was with Turner when the time came. Turner had slept well and eaten a hearty breakfast around 7 am. When it was time Turner submitted quietly to the pinioning still protesting his innocence. Throughout, his demeanour remained calm, as it had during the trial. At five minutes to eight, the crowd was large, all anxiously waiting for the hoisting of the flag. At eight o'clock on a signal from the governor Major Lane, the executioner Billington placed the noose around the prisoner's neck and released the lever. When Billington tried to put the white cap on his head Turner protested 'don't put that on. I don't want it!' Billington ignored Turner's request and put the white cap on his head. He then allowed the condemned man to drop 8 feet.

The clanging of the trap door against the side of the pit declared that Turner was no more. It appeared that death was instantaneous The black flag slowly moved up the flag-staff. As the prison bells chimed the hour a large cheer came from the crowd, showing that the execution had been carried out to the satisfaction of the public.

After the execution, Turner's body was kept in a wooden shed about midway between the central building of the prison and the house of the execution. It was laid on a raised board. On the floor was Turner's coffin. An inspection of the neck showed that the execution had been carried out dexterously. The throat was swollen and black, and there was a very slight abrasion to the skin, otherwise, there were no marks to indicate how the death occurred.

As was customary the body had been left one hour before it was cut down. Under the provisions of the Capital Punishment Act, an inquest into the execution had to take place. The original jury was required to inspect the body and the execution house. After due inspection, the jury confirmed that they were satisfied that the execution had been properly conducted in accordance with the law.

David Waterhouse and his wife travelled by train from Horsforth to Armley Gaol. Their presence at Armley was not generally known and therefore attracted a moderate share of attention. They must have felt a desire that retribution should overtake the man who had so cruelly robbed them of their daughter. As the black flag rose to view, the parents were heard to give expression to their feelings in a language of some force.

R.I.P Barabara Whitian Waterhouse.

13

A SORDID AFFAIR — EMILY SWANN & JOHN GALLAGHER THE WOMBWELL MURDERS 1903

Emily Swann and John Gallagher. (Author's own collection)

Mother of eleven, forty-two-year-old Emily Swann was a colourful character. Described as a stocky, short well-built woman with a round face, a vicious mouth and a violent temper, Emily was married to William Swann a forty-one-year-old glassblower at Aldham Glassworks by trade. The Swann's marriage was volatile from the beginning and the couple's frequent rows were legendary amongst the residents at Alma Place, George Street, Wombwell where the couple lived with their children.

In July 1901, Emily had a violent row with one of her neighbours, Eleanor Herrington. Apparently, Herrington had witnessed an earlier argument between Emily and her husband which had turned quite nasty and the police had become involved. In an attempt to avoid more trouble from the police Emily confronted Herrington, asking if she would be 'shopping her to the police' and 'You are not gonna summon arr Bill arr you?' Herrington replied, 'No I don't want owt to do with it or with you!' Emily didn't believe her neighbour and struck her a violent blow to her head with a poker rendering her unconscious for at least half an hour. The poor woman had a fractured skull, the blow breaking her nose and disfiguring her for life.

Emily Swann was arrested and admitted: 'I have done it and I will suffer for it.'

When the case came to trial Emily said in her defence, was that she had acted in self-defence after Herrington struck her first with a poker. The judge was not impressed and Emily was sentenced to six months hard labour.

Following Emily's prison sentence the couple separated for a while but soon got back together. Like many other people at the time money was tight so the Swann's took in a lodger. Thirty-year-old John Gallagher a colliery labourer who worked at Mitchell Main and he had lodged at the Swann's for six months but left due to the couple's constant arguments and also Mr Swann's jealousy. William Swann was convinced that his wife and Gallagher were having an affair. He wasn't wrong.

Gallagher and William Swann had many quarrels, but not as many as Emily and William. They argued daily, Gallagher got fed up with it. One day he saw William throw a teapot at his wife and he struck her across the face. That was enough for Gallagher so he left the couple's house and went to lodge across the street with Mary Ann Ward. He did, however, keep returning to see Emily.

On Saturday 6th June 1903 the Swanns' arguments came to a permanent end.

Emily Swann and John Gallager had been drinking for most of the day at Mary Ann Ward's house. After a couple of drinks, Gallagher and Swann went over the road to Emily's house, supposedly to retrieve some papers and a pawn ticket that Gallagher had supposedly left behind, they were both coming down the stairs when William Swann returned home. William was incensed and convinced that the couple had been fornicating upstairs in his house. An argument started between them all, and Gallagher walked off back to Mary Ward's house. Emily stayed arguing with her husband but soon ran over the road to tell Gallagher what had happened. She had a cloth over her eyes telling them that William had punched her in the face. 'Look, Johnny, see what our Bill's done!' Gallagher was enraged and yelled ' I will give him it, he can hit a woman, but he can't hit a man.'

'I hope he punches him to death, the bastard' Emily Swann was heard to say.

Gallagher had threatened William Swann many times before, telling him in no uncertain terms that 'he would get him ready for his coffin.'

John Gallagher ran over the road and a fight started between him and William Swann. Gallagher punched Swann with such force, striking him on the head and on the back of the neck. He knocked Swann down on the floor, and kicked him forcefully, then as Swann tried to get back up Gallagher took an armchair and smashed it against the fender then smashed the broken chair arm on Swann's head yelling obscenities of every kind at him. Gallagher, seeing Swann sink to the floor, ran out of the house back over the road to Mrs Ward's house, his face smeared in blood.

Emily Swann stayed with her husband and tried to get him up and put him in a chair. She tried to give him some water but he wouldn't take it and he fell back down on the floor.

Emily then went and joined her lover and friend over the road. Emily told them that Gallagher had half-killed her husband. A drunken Mrs Ward said 'I'm sick of all this, I want nothing to do with it!'

Emily turned to Gallager and said, 'You have almost killed him, he's dying.'

'Good, serves him right, I have smashed him in four ribs, I will give him a bit more to go to his grave with before I go to Bradford tonight!' Gallager then went upstairs to wash his face.

In the meantime, Emily Swann had checked on her husband and returned to Mary Ward's house in a state of panic.

Can you come over with me? I think he's dead, he won't move.' She pleaded to her friend.

Reluctantly, Mary Ward went across the road to the Swann's house and was greeted with a gruesome sight.

William Swann was indeed dead, lying lifeless on the floor his head squashed between a cupboard and a chair. A poker lay on the floor. For some reason Emily did not call the police, she waited an hour then called for Dr Foley, who pronounced William dead. The police were then called. Unfortunately, Emily was so drunk that the police could not gain any information from her, and they had to wait until the following day to get her statement.

The same evening that William Swann died one of Mary Ward's sons saw John Gallagher walking towards the local pub, the son told him that William Swann was dead. Alarmingly, Gallagher's response was not what would have been expected under the circumstances, his reply was: 'I don't care' then he started laughing loudly and began to dance in the street. 'I'm not guilty,' he shouted.

Gallagher met up with Emily, who confirmed that her husband was indeed dead. At that time she had not called for the doctor or the police, which gave John some time to disappear and go on the run from the police.

A wanted poster was soon circulated for the arrest of John Gallagher describing his features and exactly what he was wearing on the day he went missing. It was believed that he had gone to Bradford. Officers were dispatched to the area but Gallagher wasn't found. It then came to light that he had gone to Sheffield and police enquiries were made in that area.

An inquest into the murder opened on 10th June at The Horse Shoe Hotel in Wombwell. Once again the coroner was Mr Wightman. A large crowd had gathered outside the pub, police were concerned that there could be a disturbance, but the crowd was reasonably well-behaved.

The first witness to be called was the deceased's widow, Emily Swann, who created excitement in the crowd, none of whom displayed any respect for her. In dramatic fashion, she appeared with a bandage over her right eye.

In her statement, she repeated what had happened during that fateful day. She said that her husband was sober that day, as was she although he had a gill of beer at lunchtime when she was cleaning. A gasp and heads shook throughout the crowd at this statement, all her neighbours knew that Emily Swann was very rarely sober and certainly wasn't that day. Emily, hearing this, looked around the crowd narrowing her eyes, and added, 'I did get hoppled a bit later, as I was frightened.'

Dr George Ernest Atkins conducted the post mortem examination He found several bruises on the right temple, the right cheekbone and upper part of the chest. The covering of the brain was congested with blood clots in both parts of the brain and also at the base of the skull, although the skull was not fractured. The cause of death was attributed to an effusion of blood on the brain. The assistant coroner added that a great deal of violence must have been asserted on Mr Swann to cause such horrendous injuries, there were twenty in all inflicted with great force from either a blunt instrument or a boot or both.

After several witnesses had given their evidence the judge summed up and the jury retired to discuss their findings, they returned with a verdict of wilful murder against John Gallagher. However, the jury wished to call attention to the remark made by Mrs Emily Swann to John Gallagher 'I hope he punches him to death'. This statement posed the question of whether Mrs Swann should also be tried for murder.

The coroner agreed that this indeed was a good question. However, the purpose of this initial enquiry was to ascertain the deceased's cause of death and who was the alleged perpetrator. The jury had unanimously concluded it was Gallagher. The inquest then closed.

William Swann's funeral took place on On 11th June 1902. Several thousand people assembled in the vicinity of George Street and Wombwell Cemetery. The police and the local authority had taken every precaution to keep the morbid and the nosy away from the funeral except for those taking part in the procession.

A large crowd had gathered outside the Swanns' house at Alma Square, most of them women whose feelings against Emily Swann were high and the police feared that a disturbance might take place. The space outside the house was packed and even the hearse and family mourners found it difficult to find a space.

Emily was advised that due to the animosity towards her it was not a good idea for her to attend her husband's funeral and that it was safer for her to stay at home. However, Emily was not one to keep quiet for long and as the cortege began to depart Emily opened the bedroom window and addressed the crowd: 'Let him go quietly will you!'

The crowd were very antagonistic towards her and Emily soon closed the window. Still not able to resist, as soon as the hearse began to move she was seen waving vigorously through the window.

Around forty workers from Aldham Glass Company proceeded the coffin, carrying a beautiful wreath. Amongst family mourners were three daughters, two sons, and three brothers.

John Gallagher was arrested at Middlesborough on 4th August. Where he, together with Emily Swann, were taken to court and briskly marched up between two police officers to stand near the solicitor's table, to the glare of a crowded courtroom.

John Gallagher looked shabby, his clothes appeared to have weathered the storms of many winters and the sun of many summers. His black hair was unkempt and he had not shaved.

Emily was respectfully dressed in mourning black, but she wore a look of defiance on her white face. On this occasion, the hearing was adjourned to a later date in order that further evidence could be gathered. The two prisoners were escorted by train back to gaol.

The rain fell heavily over Barnsley on 18th August 1903 but did not deter a large crowd appearing outside Barnsley West Riding Police Court, where a special sitting of the magistrates was held. Gallagher and Swann were to be on trial for murder.

Both prisoners looked haggard, especially Gallagher who followed the proceedings anxiously.

As soon as Emily Swann entered the dock she folded her arms and constantly listened to what was being said, occasionally glancing around the courtroom, but not acknowledging anyone she knew.

Neither prisoner was legally represented. The case was heard and the evidence presented before the jury.

Interestingly, evidence given by Gallagher at the time of his arrest implicated that it was, in fact, Emily Swann who delivered the blow. When arrested Gallagher said to the detective, 'I may as well tell the truth, I never used the poker, but the woman did. I should know I was there at the time.'

An important witness came forward, a Mr John William Dunn a miner who lived directly opposite the Swanns and from his house he could see directly into their kitchen. At six o'clock on the day in question, he saw Gallagher standing outside the Swanns' door. The door was locked, but Emily Swann shook it violently and it flew open. Gallagher went inside, and the witness heard Gallagher shout 'I will coffin the bastard before morning.' The door was then closed and a scuffle took place inside during which Emily Swann was heard to shout 'Give it to the bastard, Johnny!' This went on for five or ten minutes, then Gallagher came outside and went over to Mrs Ward's. Gallagher then came back to the Swanns' and the same fracas happened again. This time Gallagher shouted, 'I will murder the swine before morning.' Emily was also repeating the same words she had said before.

When Gallagher came out of the house he and Emily Swann were holding hands and Gallagher had blood running down his face.

Dunn also said that the month before he had witnessed Mrs Swann knock her husband to the floor with a poker. To which Emily Swann took offence, and shouted, 'Oh man alive, I never!'

Dunn took no notice of Emily's outburst and continued giving evidence looking Emily straight in the eye when he said, 'I saw Gallagher leave the Swanns' house three or four times a week when her husband was at work, often in the early hours of the morning.'

When asked if they wanted to respond to any of this evidence, Gallagher shook his head and said no, while Emily said, 'No, I will leave him in God's hands.'

A friend of Gallagher's, John Taylor, said he had advised his friend to stay away from the Swanns as they were both bad news. Gallagher had defended Emily saying 'oh she's alright when she's sober'.

Police Sergeant Minty who had been the officer who visited the Swanns' house on the night of the murder said that both Mrs Swann and Mrs Ward were so drunk that he could not get any sense out of either of them. All Mrs Swann kept repeating was 'He's not dead, he can't be dead'.

Both prisoners were remanded in custody until December when the case was to come to trial at Leeds Assizes.

At this trial, Emily Swann's fourteen-year-old daughter wanted to give evidence as to her mother's character to say she was a good mother. However, the judge dismissed this saying, 'I doubt that you know as much as I do about this wretched woman.'

Once again the evidence was repeated. The prosecution addressed the jury to say that the facts of the murder could not be disputed. Mr

Swann died as a result of an act of violence against him but was that violence inflicted by one or two assailants?

Mr Mitchell Innes representing Galagher addressed the jury requesting that they return a verdict of manslaughter. He argued that Gallagher was not in a good state of mind when he committed this crime. He was drunk, and he was angry and inflamed with a misguided love for his lover Emily Swann. He had seen his lover being struck by her husband and he wanted to avenge her. He didn't think that it was right for him to be striking his wife.

Mr Newell addressed the jury on behalf of Emily Swann, saying that she was the mother of eleven children ranging from age twenty-two down to four. Her conduct had been reprehensible, wicked, irresponsible and stupid, but it had not been proved that she inflicted any violence towards her husband. It was alleged that she had enticed Gallagher to do what he did. Undoubtedly, she had used language that she should not have used, but he requested that the jury not convict her on a short temper and intemperate words. The cause of Mr Swann's death was not the work of a woman, her actions showed that she didn't want her husband dead, rather she wanted him to have a good thumping for what he did to her.

His Lordship summed up the evidence, reminding the jury that their job was not to shrink from their duties, it was for them to decide if the prisoners were innocent or guilty, and if guilty were they both or singularly guilty of murder or manslaughter?

The jury retired and returned half an hour later to deliver their verdict. 'Guilty' against both prisoners.

His Lordship issued the death sentence in the usual form against both prisoners.

Both Swann and Gallagher were unmoved by the verdict. When asked if they wanted to say anything Gallagher shook his head. Emily, on the other hand, said, 'I am not afraid of immediate death, as I know that I am innocent, and I will go to God.'

On her way down the stairs of the courtroom, Emily Swann recognised someone in the gallery. She smiled and kissed both her hands and shook them violently at the people she had seen.

After their conviction, there was a great deal of indifference between the two prisoners. Gallagher accepted that he would not be reprieved and accepted his fate calmly. Friends that visited him said he was quite jovial and chatty. Whereas Emily was convinced that she would be reprieved and had appealed her sentence. However, the Home Secretary denied her request. When she received the home office decision she became violently hysterical, and her grief and despair were acute. She rallied against her sentence and bitterly blamed Gallagher for bringing her to this dreadful state of affairs.

Did Emily Swann deserve to die, was she a hard-faced murderer who had an adulterous affair and persuaded her lover to kill her husband, or was she simply a woman, the mother of eleven children who had been pushed to the limit through years of drunken violence and every day beatings at the hands of her husband? Whilst waiting for her fate at Armley Gaol she became popular with her keepers. Her family visited her frequently, she did not write to her eighty-year-old mother. She thought it would be all too much for her.

On the morning of the execution, Emily Swann was overwrought with emotion. The wardens brought her a glass of brandy and she soon regained her composure as best she could. A few days before she had repented and admitted her guilt in the crime to the prison chaplain, and accepted that her sentence was just. The chaplain gave her communion on the morning of her death. She had made her peace with God and prepared herself to her inevitable fate.

Billington was again the executioner and it was agreed that the couple were to be hanged together. This was the first and last time a woman was hanged at Armley Gaol.

The night before their fate both prisoners slept well. The following morning with the exception of the white hat both prisoners wore their ordinary clothes. Punctually, at nine o'clock, the solemn procession from the condemned cell to the scaffold began. The prison chaplain and Reverend Mansell led the way reciting prayers from The Burial Service.

Gallagher was guarded on both sides by a prison warden, his hands pinioned behind his back. Followed by Emily Swann guarded by two female wardresses. Both prisoners regained a calm demeanour. Just before they reached the scaffold Emily turned around to Gallagher and in a cheery voice said, 'Morning, John.'

At first, Gallagher appeared startled, but he soon regained his self-possession, he replied in a clear voice. 'Good morning, love.'

These were the only words that passed between the pair on the way or on the scaffold. Billington did not prolong the drama and adjusted the caps and tightened the ropes. Then there was a click and the bolt was drawn, and the two murderers passed into eternity.

The coroner confirmed that both deaths were instantaneous and were 'perfectly painless in both cases!' The jury then confirmed that justice had been done and the murderers were executed in the terms of the verdict.

Both Emily Swann and John Gallagher were buried within the walls of Armley Gaol.

References

Barnsley Chronicle, May 1902. Emily Swann & John
Hull Daily Mail, 18th August 1891, Emily Swann
Illustrated Weekly News, 14th March 1868, Miles Weatherhill.
Leeds Intelligencer, 24 April 1847, Armley Gaol
Sheffield Evening Telegraph, 29th December 1888, John Gill
Sheffield Independent, 11th February 1882, Kate Dover
Yorkshire Evening Post, 27, November 1894, Samuel Stonehouse.
Yorkshire Gazette, 2nd November 1889, John Gill
Yorkshire Gazette, 1st January 1848, The Mirfield Murders

Thank you to Gary Peacock, and The Mirfield History Archive Facebook group.

ABOUT THE AUTHOR

Wendy was born in Yorkshire in the late 1950s. She moved to the coastal town of Filey in North Yorkshire with her husband and family in the middle 1990s. She has a BA Hons degree in English Literature and a Master's degree in Creative Writing.

Wendy has had many jobs from working in a library, a bank, a financial advisor, and owning her own bar and restaurant.

Her first book Filey, a History of The Town and its People, traces the history of the town from Roman times and the Norman Conquest.

Her second book Dr Pritchard The Poisoning Adulterer retells the terrible story of the Victorian Doctor Edward William Pritchard. The book is written creatively, and effectively brings the doctor and his family back to life. All events in the book are true and are meticulously researched.

Scarborough a History of the Town and its People traces the history of Scarborough through the years from its origins in the ice age to the finding of Spa waters to it's becoming Britain's first seaside resort.

Printed in Poland
by Amazon Fulfillment
Poland Sp. z o.o., Wrocław

54997997R00078